UNDERSTANDING

YOUR

Suicide
Grief

[SECOND EDITION]

UNDERSTANDING
YOUR
Suicide Grief

TEN ESSENTIAL TOUCHSTONES
FOR FINDING HOPE AND
HEALING YOUR HEART

[SECOND EDITION]

ALAN D. WOLFELT, PH.D.

Companion
PRESS

Fort Collins, Colorado
An imprint of the Center for Loss and Life Transition

Companion
P R E S S

Companion Press is dedicated to the education and support
of both the bereaved and bereavement caregivers. We believe that those
who companion the bereaved by walking with them as they journey in
grief have a wondrous opportunity: to help others embrace and
grow through grief—and to lead fuller, more deeply-lived lives
themselves because of this important ministry.

For a complete catalog and ordering information, write or call:

Companion Press
The Center for Loss and Life Transition
3735 Broken Bow Road
Fort Collins, CO 80526
(970) 226-6050
www.centerforloss.com

First edition, ISBN 978-1-87965-158-6 © 2009 by Alan D. Wolfelt, Ph.D.

Second edition, ISBN 978-1-61722-335-8 © 2024 by Alan D. Wolfelt, Ph.D.

Companion Press is an imprint of the
Center for Loss and Life Transition
3735 Broken Bow Road
Fort Collins, Colorado 80526

Printed in the United States of America

30 29 28 27 26 25 24   5 4 3 2 1

ISBN: 978-1-61722-335-8

To the thousands of suicide loss survivors who have invited me to walk with them through the wilderness of their grief.

What you have taught me I attempt teach to others.

Thank you for entrusting me to "companion" not "treat" you; to "care" for you, not "cure" you.

I am humbled to be able to provide hospitality to you through this resource as you allow yourselves to openly, honestly, and authentically mourn.

The *Understanding Your Suicide Grief* Series

SECOND EDITION

This book is designed to be used along with
The Understanding Your Suicide Grief Journal, Second Edition,
also by Dr. Alan Wolfelt. There is also a support group facilitator
guide available entitled *The Understanding Your Suicide Grief
Support Group Guide, Second Edition*.

Contents

TOUCHSTONE THREE
Embrace the Uniqueness of Your Grief | 63

TOUCHSTONE FOUR

Explore Your Feelings of Loss | 85

TOUCHSTONE SEVEN

Nurture Yourself | 179

Foreword

Honored – that's the word that first came to mind when Dr. Wolfelt asked us to write a foreword to the Second Edition of *Understanding Your Suicide Grief.* This was followed by Humbled – our mentor and friend is asking us to write this. For us, it has been, and continues to be, a privilege to learn from the man considered by many to be North America's leading expert on grief (though he understandably cringes at being considered an "expert").

We first began our grief journey with the loss of our son, Drey, in 2012. He was a handsome, athletic 19-year-old who had just graduated high school a few months earlier with lots of friends and a loving family. He had recently purchased a car that he had been wanting and was talking about college. That August morning had begun just like the one before it. Who could've known that our life was about to radically change.

One of the things you will read in this book concerns the movement of grief, the transition of our relationship from one of presence to one of memory. The death of Drey was like being evicted from the one and forced into the other. This isn't what we wanted; we didn't sign up for this. Although we were blessed to have many friends and family to support us, it was still difficult to express just how deep our pain was. Many of the kind gestures and words of condolence felt lacking, they didn't really know what we were going through. They meant well but we still felt very alone.

Then, in 2014, we began a non-profit to support those who were bereaved by suicide. Of course, we wanted to learn as much as we could, and this inevitably led us to Dr. Alan Wolfelt and the Center for Loss and Life Transition. It was there we learned the principles of his companioning model and knew that this was a perfect fit for our vision and calling. His companioning model, the underlying foundation of this book, provided the missing piece for us. This is what was lacking from so many well-meaning efforts of friends and family. We didn't need on-lookers to our grief, we needed someone to walk beside us in our grief.

We were immediately drawn to Dr. Wolfelt's writings and continue to admire him, not just because of the wisdom he shares, but because he is a lifelong learner. We appreciate his openness and curiosity about people's grief experiences and how he incorporates this into his expanding body of knowledge. It was especially evident as we took his training classes. Watching him employ the practices of companioning made the material come alive.

We began providing support groups using *Understanding Your Suicide Grief*. We were trained in and familiar with other support group models, but they didn't seem to connect in the same way. As loss survivors ourselves, we knew what we were looking for in a group and the principles found in *Understanding Your Suicide Grief* were it.

And while this book is certainly valuable to the individual, engaging its content with others in a group setting can help bring further nuance to its application. We recommend using this book in conjunction with the journal and facilitator guide. The valuable content can also be used in other ways. Topics such as "the six needs of mourning" or "the misconceptions of suicide grief" can easily be used as stand-alone sessions in any group setting. The accompanying journal is a fantastic companion. Even if someone doesn't like to write, the questions and discussion points help to enrich the content immeasurably.

We began with just one group. Soon, we were doing nine groups throughout the year with several facilitators, many of which had been participants in previous groups. Their group experience, mentorship, and the facilitator guide from Dr. Wolfelt helped prepare them. Several participants attended more than one group. Each time, they spoke of getting more out of the book than before.

Participants' reactions within our groups were positive, but that's not to say they didn't wrestle with parts. As we came to the end of a group and began talking about seeking integration and appreciating our transformation, many were not ready to hear that. We would always encourage them – and we encourage you – don't give up on it. You may not be ready to hear these things right now, but you will in your timing. Use them as beacons to help guide you through your wilderness of grief.

To say these groups were successful would be an understatement. In our experience we have seen hundreds, if not thousands, of lives touched and renewed by the principles found in this book. Suicide loss support groups and Dr. Wolfelt's *Understanding Your Suicide Grief* book continue to reach and encourage those bereaved by a suicide loss. The valuable updates in this second edition demonstrate his ongoing commitment to support grieving people.

Dr. Wolfelt describes grief as a wilderness, and it is. Vastly unexplored and unknown to us, we desperately search for direction in a place where all the trees look the same. No one would want to make such a journey alone without a guide, someone to point out the trail and help us navigate it. Through this book, Dr. Wolfelt points out the trail markers and provides hope that we can make this journey, both for ourselves and as we journey with others.

Robbie Graham
Denise Meine-Graham, C.T. TRCC
Postvention Consulting, LLC
Postventionconsulting.com

Welcome
An Invitation to Open Your Heart

Someone you care about has died by suicide. You are heartbroken, and your entire being literally aches physically, cognitively, emotionally, socially, and spiritually. You may well feel alone, isolated, and dazed.

You are no doubt hurting and in search of understanding, compassion, and solace. My sincere hope is that you will find all of these in the following pages. Thank you for allowing me to companion you on your journey. I too have walked this path and realize you have been "torn apart" and, just like me, have some very "unique needs."

"No rule book. No time frame. Grief is as individual as a fingerprint. Do what is right for your soul."

Unknown

Even as a child I could see that our culture doesn't do grief well. In fact, it was then that I decided when I grew up (I wrote my mission statement at age 16), I would try to be a force for change and an advocate for grieving people. I would make it my life's work to evolve our culture's understanding of grief and how to support one another after a loss.

And so, it came to be that I found my calling at a young age. I focused my energy on becoming a thanatologist (a fancy word for grief counselor) and death educator. In 1985 I founded the Center for Loss and Life Transition. My specific passion for supporting suicide loss survivors was inspired by the death of one of my best friends.

When my good friend Ken took his life, my personal and professional life was transformed forever.

Following Ken's death I felt the need to write the first edition of this book (2009). Prior to that I had supported many people who had someone they care deeply about die by suicide. Yet, I found myself totally humbled in the face of my own loss. The wound of my grief gave birth to being an advocate for suicide loss survivors. I'm so grateful that the first edition of *Understanding Your Suicide Grief* has reached hundreds of thousands of grievers, and, together with its companion journal, continues to be used as the resource for many suicide grief support groups.

This year I decided it was time for an update. Since 2009 I have learned a great deal more from survivors and I have taught a number of trainings on this critically important topic. This second edition of *Understanding Your Suicide Grief* contains a number of what I hope are helpful additions.

Concurrently, I've updated the *Understanding Your Suicide Grief Journal* and *The Understanding Your Suicide Grief Support Group Guide*. So the page numbers and the topics align, I encourage you to use the second editions of these resources as well.

I'm also gratified to report that since the time I was a grieving teen, and especially during the last two decades since the publication of the first *Understanding Your Suicide Grief*, our culture has gotten a bit better at acknowledging and supporting people in grief. While we still have a way to go, I've seen progress. We're awakening to mental health issues and the idea of holistic wellness. We're beginning to leave behind dated, harmful constructs about what it means to "be strong." We're developing more emotional intelligence and are more apt to talk openly about losses and the difficult feelings that naturally go hand-in-hand with them. We're appreciating, more and more, the importance of good self-care during naturally difficult times in our lives.

Acknowledging Your Life Changing Grief

The suicide death of a friend or family member is not our choice, yet we are faced with the need to confront our raw life-changing grief. For a number of reasons, we may not know how or where or if we should express the pain that comes with this profound loss. Yet, by picking up this book when you're hurting, you're taking one small step toward integrating this loss into your life. The good news is that **grief responds to attention and expression.** I often say that **grief waits on welcome, not on time.**

SUICIDE IN THE UNITED STATES (2022 Statistics)

- Suicide was the 11th leading cause of death in the United States. 49,476 Americans died by suicide.
- Men died by suicide at a rate 3.85x higher than women.
- Rates were highest among adults 85+ years old and next highest for those 75-84.
- Suicide is the second leading cause of death among young people aged 10-14, and the third leading cause of death among those 15-24 years.
- The highest age-adjusted suicide rate was among American Indians and Alaskan Natives (16.11 per 100,000 individuals) and the second highest rate was among Whites (15.83 per 100,000).
- LGBTQ+ young people are more than four times as likely to attempt suicide than their peers.
- Besides a slight decrease in 2019 and 2020, the suicide rate has increased each year since 2000.
- Suicide rates vary by both state and country. For more information on your specific location, contact your local health agency.

Sources: American Foundation for Suicide Prevention, the Center for Disease Control, and The Trevor Project.

Recent studies have noted that each suicide affects, on average, a minimum of five family members and up to 135 community members. Secondary to the fact that approximately 700,000 people worldwide die by suicide annually, it is estimated that 60 million people become suicide loss survivors each year. These numbers alone help us know how important it is to not suffer alone or in silence. You need and deserve unconditional support and compassion.

I believe it is vitally important to remember: You are not alone. Your fellow suicide loss survivors can help you. This book can help you.

SURVIVING THE EARLY DAYS

If your loss was recent, you may find that you're not yet ready to engage with the contents of this book. Feelings of shock and numbness naturally dominate early suicide grief, as does a diminished ability to concentrate. These normal responses may make it difficult, if not impossible, to read through the following touchstones and feel like you're being helped by the experience.

So, if you were given this book by a well-intentioned friend or purchased it yourself shortly after the death – only to find that you can't focus on it and it doesn't speak to your immediate needs – I encourage you to set it aside for the time being.

Instead, concentrate on doing whatever you need to do to survive, one day at a time. Breathe in and out. Turn to your friends and family members. Comfort yourself however you can. Reach out to a counselor if you're finding it unbearable to make it through each day.

Later on, when the shock and psychic numbness start to wear off and you're regaining the capacity to focus, pick up this book and the companion journal again. I believe they can help you, but it's a matter of timing. Go at your own pace and come back whenever you're ready.

And, with some vital education, your friends and family members can help you. Yes, there is help, and there is hope.

As a result of fear and misunderstanding, many of us as survivors of suicide are often left alone and in silence when we desperately need unconditional support and understanding. As a suicide loss survivor, I discovered firsthand that we suffer in a variety of ways: one, because we need to mourn the loss of someone significant in our life; two, because we have experienced a sudden, usually unexpected traumatic death; and three, because we are at risk for being shunned by a society unwilling to enter into the pain of our grief. What we need and deserve is unconditional love, not shame or judgment.

I truly hope this book provides you some of the unconditional love you need right now in your life. All too many people suffer the trauma of suicide grief in isolation. **Yet we all need companions if we are to survive and eventually rekindle our own life force.** Again, I hope this book becomes a reliable companion into and through the ten Touchstones that follow.

The Ten Touchstones

This brings us to the concept of the "touchstones" that I believe you will find helpful in your journey. I have used the concept of touchstones in the book because it speaks to my heart. By definition, a touchstone is a standard or norm against which to measure something. In this book I describe ten touchstones, or benchmarks. I explore these touchstones with you not only because they have helped the survivors of suicide I have had the honor of companioning, but they have also been helpful to me in my own experience.

TOUCHSTONE ONE   Open to the Presence of Your Loss

TOUCHSTONE TWO   Dispel Misconceptions About Grief

TOUCHSTONE THREE   Embrace the Uniqueness of Your Grief

TOUCHSTONE FOUR	Explore Your Feelings of Loss
TOUCHSTONE FIVE	Understand the Six Needs of Mourning
TOUCHSTONE SIX	Recognize You Are Not Crazy
TOUCHSTONE SEVEN	Nurture Yourself
TOUCHSTONE EIGHT	Reach Out for Help
TOUCHSTONE NINE	Seek Reconcilition, Not Resolution
TOUCHSTONE TEN	Appreciate Your Transformation

Think of your grief as a wilderness—a vast, mountainous, inhospitable forest. You are in the wilderness now. You are in the midst of unfamiliar and often brutal surroundings. You are cold and tired. You must journey through this wilderness. Yet, as you do so with the help of this resource, remember: go slowly. There are no rewards for speed! Basic wilderness training teaches us, "When you get lost, stay put. Wait and call out for help." As you slowly find your way out of this wilderness experience, you must become acquainted with its terrain and learn to follow the sometimes hard-to-find trail that leads to healing.

In the wilderness of your grief, the touchstones are your trail markers. They are the signs that let you know you are on the right path. I also like to think of them as "wisdom teachings" that the many people I have supported following a suicide death have taught me.

Those who have gone before you and I have indeed left us many trail markers that show us how they made it through the wilderness of suicide grief. If we look, we will see that they have been gracious enough to pass them on to others who enter this inhospitable wilderness. I feel an obligation to teach what they as fellow travelers have taught me. Again, you and I are not alone. Others have gone before us and discovered the strength not only to survive, but eventually to thrive. From the depths of my being, I believe you can too!

And even when you've become a master journeyer and you know well the terrain of your grief, you will at times feel like you are backtracking and being ravaged by the forces around you. This, too, is the nature of grief after a death to suicide. Complete mastery of a wilderness is not possible. Just as we cannot control the winds and the storms and the beasts in nature, we can never have total dominion over our grief.

But if you do the work of mourning, if you become an intrepid traveler on your journey, if you make use of these ten touchstones, I promise you that you will find your way out of the wilderness of your grief and you will learn to have renewed meaning and purpose in your precious life.

EXPRESS YOURSELF:
Go to *The Understanding Your Suicide Grief Journal* on p. 10.

Understanding as Surrendering

The title of this book is *Understanding Your Suicide Grief*. But there is a paradox in the concept of "understanding" suicide grief. You see, it is instinctive to want to understand or figure out the "why?" of the suicide of someone we love. Yet, it is this very need to totally understand that can get us into trouble. When we are confronted with suicide, we face a mystery. It is not possible to know exactly what goes on in the head and heart of a person before he or she dies by suicide—it is a mystery. And, as someone once astutely observed, "Mystery is not something to be explained, it is something to be pondered." The starting point for the instinctive "why?" must be anchored in a confession of mystery.

Sometimes we simply cannot understand the suicide death of someone we have cared about so deeply. Yet we often ask, "why did this happen?" on the pathway to "how will I survive the reality that it did happen?" Do not shame yourself if you struggle with the "why?"; it is organic, instinctive, and often rooted in wanting back a person whom we valued. But in the end, suicide is an act of solitude.

We often cannot understand why a person we care so much about would choose death in this way. I certainly couldn't understand why my friend Ken chose to die. I didn't understand—I protested as a natural part of my grief. While Ken's death by suicide remains a mystery, **I do not care any less about him because of his choice than I would have had the circumstances of his death been different.**

I have found that sometimes it is in staying open to the mystery and recognizing that we don't understand and can't control everything that some level of understanding comes. In fact, perhaps it is "standing under" the mysterious experience of suicide grief that provides us with a unique perspective. Maybe only after exhausting an instinctive search for the "why" of suicide can we discover a newly defined "why" for our own lives.

My personal and professional experience suggests that right when you are in the midst of your own questioning, some well-intentioned, misinformed people may come along and ask, "Why did they commit suicide?"

It's not enough that we are often asking this ourselves; those whom I call the "voyeuristically curious" often feel compelled to question this as well. While some people can respond to the issue of "why" with clarity and conviction, most of us find it difficult to answer clearly. (Of course, we know that the use of the word "commit" – while common – is inappropriate. For more on the language of suicide, see page 19.)

Again, it's instinctive to ponder the question, but don't think you should have the answer! The grief that suicide brings has its own voice and should not be compromised by our need for complete understanding. Surrender can actually help you unleash your capacity to openly and authentically mourn. Breathe. Give attention to what you need to give attention to. Hold this mystery in your heart and surround yourself with caring, compassionate companions who sit with you in unconditional love and make no judgment on where you are in the journey. I encourage you to surrender to your work of mourning.

EXPRESS YOURSELF:
Go to *The Understanding Your Suicide Grief Journal* on p. 11.

WHAT DO YOU TELL OTHER PEOPLE ABOUT THE SUICIDE?

While our society is seeing some positive changes, there continues to be a tremendous amount of taboo and stigma surrounding suicide. For various reasons, some families decide to keep the circumstances of the death a secret or inform people that it was another cause of death. In addition, some families attempt to conceal the cause of death (particularly from children) believing it will insulate family members and friends from a reality that is too painful to bear.

In my forty years of experience, truth-telling is my best counsel. Lying and trying to mislead about the cause of death only makes it worse. We as humans can often cope with what we know, not what we don't know. The majority of suicide loss survivors I have had the honor of supporting are glad that they decided to tell the truth.

The advantages of telling the truth: 1) when families and friends know the truth, they become more able to provide the support to each other that they need and deserve; 2) there is no concern that people (particularly children) will learn about the suicide from someone outside the family; 3) there is no drain of emotional and spiritual energy on projecting some form of denial; 4) you don't have to try to remember who knows the truth and who doesn't; and 5) you are befriending the most vital need of mourning – acknowledging the reality of the death.

As you acknowledge the reality of the suicide death, you are also helping combat some of the societal stigma and taboo

(Continued on next page.)

surrounding it. Some of the following honest and direct expressions may well be appropriate for you:

"He died by suicide after a long-time struggle with depression."

"She died by suicide. We don't understand why but we continue to love her."

"My husband died by suicide after struggling with PTSD following his time serving our country."

When people pose questions you don't care to answer (which sometimes may occur), the following can be a way to respond:

"That is not something I'm prepared to talk about right now. I just need to know I have your support as I allow myself to mourn."

"I don't have a need to talk about the specific details about how he died. But thank you for your concern."

"I know when you asked that question you were trying to understand what happened to her. But right now I just need your support, not your questions."

Remember – you have the right to provide supportive confrontation to people that are making statements or asking questions that you are not prepared to answer. You have the right to choose with whom you express your thoughts and feelings.

Finding Hope

Through the experiences of walking with and learning from thousands of suicide loss survivors (and surviving my own personal walk), I want to emphasize the following truths:

You are not to blame, you can and will survive this wilderness experience, and you do not have to go through this alone.

Yes, you do have unique needs and are suffering as you sit in the wound of your loss. Yet you cannot only look forward to healing, you can look forward to going on to eventually enjoy life again.

SITTING IN YOUR WOUNDS

This is about surrendering to your grief in recognition that the only way to the other side is through. This acknowledges you are willing to do the work that mourning requires. Paradoxically, this befriending of your wound is what eventually restores your life and your living. To do this requires that you do not shut the world out, but let the world come in.

The contents of this book are anchored in the foundation of hope. **Hope is an expectation of a good that is yet to be.** It is an expression of the present alive with the possible. It is a belief that healing can and will occur. In honoring the ten touchstones, you are making an effort to find hope for your continued life, living, and loving. Through intentional mourning, you yourself can be the purveyor of your hope. You create hope in yourself by actively mourning the death and setting your intention to heal.

When you feel hopeless, frustrated, and are struggling (and you no doubt will at times), you can also challenge yourself to reach out to others for help. Spend time with others who have walked this walk and who affirm your need to mourn yet at the same time give you hope for healing. People who are empathetic, nonjudgmental, good listeners and who model positive, optimistic ways of being in the world will be your best companions. They will help resupply you with hope when your stores are running low. They will help you build divine momentum toward your eventual exodus from the wilderness of your grief.

EXPRESS YOURSELF:
Go to *The Understanding Your Suicide Grief Journal* on p. 12.

DIVINE MOMENTUM

Now and then in this book you'll hear me talk about "divine momentum" in the grief journey. This is the experience of being propelled toward healing by doing what is helpful and necessary.

Sometimes after you've actively worked on one of the six needs of mourning (see page 135), you may notice that you feel a bubble of hope or buoyed by a sense of movement toward what I call **reconciliation**. You'll realize that you are authentically befriending and expressing your grief, and, slowly and over time, healing. These moments of awareness are indicators of divine momentum.

Divine momentum is the opposite of being stuck. When you're feeling stuck in your grief journey – which will happen, too, sometimes – you can remember to turn to those mourning activities and practices that restart your divine momentum.

Healing Your Heart

An open heart that is mourning is a well of reception; it is moved entirely by what it takes in or perceives. **Authentic mourning means being totally vulnerable to what you think and feel in response to the suicide death.** Keeping your heart open wide allows you to listen to your life force, or spirit, and slowly brings you out of the dark and into the light.

You see, I have learned through experience that integrating suicide grief into our lives is heart-based, not head-based. The contents of this book encourage you to think, yes, but more importantly to feel with all your heart and soul.

The Courage to Feel Your Feelings of Loss

The word *courage* comes from the old French word for heart (*coeur*). When you're impacted so deeply by a suicide death, part of you may want to shut down your feelings or try to go around them, inhibit them, or deny them the attention they demand. The death of someone to suicide pries open your heart even if it wants to stay closed. Now, as hard as it is to do, you must open your heart, which has been engaged against its will, and muster the courage to encounter a wide range of feelings.

The word **feeling** originates from the Indo-European root and means touch. Obviously, all of us are invited to be touched by experiences we encounter along life's path—happy, sad, and everything in between. There is actually a fancy-sounding word called **perturbation** that means when we openly feel our feelings, we discover the capacity to experience change and movement.

If you cannot befriend feelings, or if you choose to deny or push them away, you become closed in your ability to use them or to be changed by them. Instead of experiencing movement, you become stuck! So, to integrate suicide grief into your life requires that you allow yourself to be touched by what you feel.

Courage also involves doing what you believe is right, despite the fact that others may strongly or persuasively disagree. For example, some of your family and friends may tell you things like, "You need to put the past in the past and move on." Instead, you have had the courage to pick up this book in an effort to better understand your unique needs related to being a suicide loss survivor. Thank you for your courage. Do not allow anyone to deny you your need to authentically mourn.

This book, directed from my heart to your heart, is an invitation to go to a spiritual place inside yourself. Doing so will allow you to enter deeply, but with self-compassion and patience, into the journey and transcend our mourning-avoidant culture. In many ways, the path of the heart is an individual exploration into the wilderness, along unmarked and unlit paths. In part, my hope in this book is to provide you some light along your path.

EXPRESS YOURSELF:
Go to *The Understanding Your Suicide Grief Journal* on p. 13.

A Word About Faith and Spirituality

Readers new to my work may wonder if this is a religious book, a nonreligious book, or something in between.

What I believe is that grief is first and foremost a spiritual journey because it forces us to examine our most fundamental beliefs and feelings about why we are here and what life means. To me, spirituality means engaging with these big questions and the deepest, most meaningful stirrings of your heart in whatever ways you choose.

While I was raised in the Methodist church, I invite all spiritual traditions, understandings, and practices to this book. You may sometimes note that I use words or concepts such as "God," "faith," "soul," or "spirit." Take or leave them as you will, and feel free to substitute your own understanding.

Whether you are deeply religious, agnostic, or atheist, you grieve and must express your grief. Pondering the meaning of life and love and the possibilities of the mysteries we do not and cannot fully understand is an essential part of your journey.

EXPRESS YOURSELF:
Go to *The Understanding Your Suicide Grief Journal* on p. 14.

Owning and Honoring Your Journey

I have attempted to convey in the following pages an active empathy, encouraging you to own your rightful role as expert of your own grief experience. You see, I have discovered a touchstone in my own personal walk into suicide grief and in my "companioning" of fellow human beings: I can only help people when I encourage them to teach me about their unique journeys.

You may consider this helping attitude strange. After all, as a professional grief counselor, am I not supposed to "treat" the person who has come to me for help? No, not really. My experience has made me aware that thinking a trained counselor like myself should have all the answers for grieving people only complicates their experience. Some traditional grief therapies tend to be controlling. The counselor is supposed to be "in charge" and to know what is best for the person in grief. However, I believe this treatment-oriented, more prescriptive approach can be harmful as opposed to helpful.

Instead, if I encourage you to be my teacher, I not only become more helpful to you, but I am enriched and changed in meaningful ways in my own life. Likewise, if you as a mourner conceive of yourself as the teacher or expert of your own grief—as the master of the journey that is your grief—you will feel empowered to own what you are feeling and not feel shamed or deterred by the sometimes judgmental responses of others. You will also learn to seek out the support of those who naturally adopt a companioning attitude toward you and avoid those who don't.

EXPRESS YOURSELF:
Go to *The Understanding Your Suicide Grief Journal* on p. 15.

COMPANIONING VERSUS TREATING

To help you feel empowered to be in charge of your own grief, please allow me to share with you a little about my grief counseling philosophy, which I call "companioning."

The word "treat" comes from the Latin root word tractare, which means "to drag." If we combine that with the word "patient," we can really get in trouble. "Patient" means "passive long-term sufferer." So if as a grief counselor I treat patients, I drag passive long-term sufferers.

On the other hand, the word "companion," when broken down into its original Latin roots means "messmate": com for "with" and pan for "bread." Someone you would share a meal with, a friend, an equal. I have taken liberties with the noun "companion" and made it into the verb "companioning" because it so well captures the type of counseling relationship

(Continued on next page.)

I support and for which I advocate. More specifically, grief counselors who embrace the companioning model understand that:

- Companioning is about being present to another person's pain; it is not about taking away the pain.

- Companioning is about going to the wilderness of the soul with another human being; it is not about thinking you are responsible for finding the way out.

- Companioning is about honoring the spirit; it is not about focusing on the intellect.

- Companioning is about listening with the heart; it is not about analyzing with the head.

- Companioning is about bearing witness to the struggles of others; it is not about judging or directing these struggles.

- Companioning is about walking alongside; it is not about leading.

- Companioning is about discovering the gifts of sacred silence; it is not about filling up every moment with words.

- Companioning is about being still; it is not about frantic movement forward.

- Companioning is about respecting disorder and confusion; it is not about imposing order and logic.

- Companioning is about learning from others; it is not about teaching them.

- Companioning is about compassionate curiosity; it is not about expertise.

I always invite—and sometimes even challenge—counselors who come to my trainings at the Center for Loss in Fort Collins, Colorado, to adopt a companioning, teach-me attitude with people in grief. When we think of ourselves as grief companions, we counselors are less likely to make inappropriate interpretations or judgments of the mourner's experiences. This approach helps ensure that when a person in grief expresses thoughts, feelings, or attitudes, we consciously avoid making evaluative reactions like, "That's right or wrong," "That shouldn't be," or worse yet, "That's pathological." Instead, all responses are valid, and everything belongs.

How to Use This Book

This book will attempt to compassionately invite you to learn about your journey into and through the grief that comes with being a suicide loss survivor. As you have without doubt already discovered, grief is an intensely personal experience. Your own grief is unlike anyone else's, even though you may find you share many commonalities with others. I hope you discover this book to be a safe place to embrace what you uniquely think and feel without fear of being judged.

As a suicide loss survivor, you have experienced a trauma loss. Trauma can be defined as an event of such intensity or magnitude that it would overwhelm any human being's capacity to cope with the demands of life. Trauma is an injury; something hurtful. It is the wounding of your emotions, your spirit, your beliefs about yourself and the world around you. It can impact your will to live, your dignity, and your sense of safety and security.

You have been traumatized by the suicide death of a family member, a friend, a coworker, a neighbor, or someone else whose life touched yours. I do not want you to experience this alone or in isolation.

How is this grief different than your response to an anticipated death? As you know, any death of those we care deeply about naturally results in painful feelings of loss and grief. But when you are faced with a suicide death, your mind has an especially difficult time acknowledging and absorbing the circumstances of the death itself.

In part, the word trauma refers to intense feelings of shock, fear, anxiety, and helplessness surrounding the cause of death. The traumatic nature of suicide and your thoughts and feeling about it will color every aspect of your grief. It is part of your grief. But it is not the totality of your grief.

Other factors that I will explore with you in this book include the nature of the relationship you had with the person who died by suicide, your unique personality, your spiritual/religious/philosophical and cultural background, your gender, your age, your personal experiences with loss, and many more. So, while there are many things that shape your grief, you can take a proactive role in your eventual healing from this trauma. In part, you are doing just that by picking up this book.

By actively engaging with this book, you are empowering yourself to do something with your grief—to mourn it, to express it outside of yourself, to find ways to help yourself heal. And you will heal. You will live and love again. Keep telling yourself, "I am not alone." Millions of others have not only survived a suicide death of someone loved, they've chosen to truly live. Find ways to reach out to these people. Find ways to share your experience. Find ways to make connections.

One way to make a connection is to interact with this book. The companion journal to this book *(The Understanding Your Suicide Grief Journal: Exploring the Ten Essential Touchstones)* gives you needed space to write out your unique thoughts and feelings. Neither this book nor the journal attempts to prescribe how you should feel but instead invite you to think and feel. While they do describe the ten essential touchstones, you will find that each of these touchstones will be lived and experienced in different ways by different people, including you.

This book and journal can also be used in conjunction with a support group. I believe that many people benefit from participation in a support group. To assist in the creation of the group, there is a resource that is part of this series titled *The Understanding Your Suicide Grief Support Group Guide.* The American Foundation for Suicide Prevention (www.afsp.org) maintains a list of survivor support groups throughout the United States and Canada.

This book is not intended to replace either a support group or personal counseling. No book, not this book or any other book, can ever replace the actual experience of moving your grief into mourning with companions who have walked the walk. No book can replace counseling for those who need it. Seeking counseling for this trauma loss is never a sign of weakness, actually it is a sign of strength.

THE LANGUAGE OF SUICIDE

The words we use in referring to suicide are critically important. They reflect our values. As we have learned more about being sensitive and compassionate to suicide loss survivors, we have seen an important movement to use the words "died by suicide" instead of "commit" to describe the act. This is because the word "commit" has been historically tied to the taboo and stigma surrounding suicide. In addition, the word "commit" is often associated with sin. Additional preferred terms are "killed himself," "took his life," or "suicided."

Some people use the phrase, "completed suicide." However, this can also be problematic. Some people think it implies that there were multiple suicide attempts that preceded the actual death, and, as you know, this is often not the case.

The term "suicide loss survivor" as used in this book refers to a person who experiences the death of a family member or friend to suicide. Some people get confused by this and think it means a person who has attempted suicide but survived. Actually, a person who attempts but does not die by suicide

(Continued on next page.)

is referred to as an "attempter" or a "survivor of a suicide attempt." I realize that some people do not like the term "suicide loss survivor," but for the sake of clarity, I chose to use it in this book. Perhaps it will help you to think of it this way: Someone you love has died, and you are now on a journey to learn how to survive the loss. You are a survivor. In fact, if you do your grief work and receive the support you need, you will not only survive, you will go on to live a life of love, meaning, and purpose.

The bottom line is that when talking about the death, you should use language that feels comfortable for you. Different people will be comfortable with different language. What feels right to you?

For many survivors, it takes months and even years to acknowledge that the death was by suicide, and during this time of reckoning, you may simply be uncomfortable with ANY language that connotes that the person took his or her own life. I understand that. I also know that part of your eventual healing involves fully acknowledging this painful reality, in your head as well as your heart. Whether you use the term "died by suicide" or the phrases "took his own life," "ended his own life," "killed himself," or "suicided," growing to accept the reality of the means of the death, and being able to admit this reality in the language you use, are essential steppingstones on your journey through the wilderness of suicide grief.

I would also note that you will find that some people, when they have not been taught the appropriate language, will, with no harm intended, use the word "commit." I would encourage you to have grace with these people for they often know not what they do. When you believe the timing is right, you can gently educate them about the appropriate language. They key is when the timing is right and when you feel up to it.

I do encourage you to complete the companion journal, whether you do it on your own, in conjunction with a support group based on this book, or with a suicide grief informed counselor. Journaling your experience can be a powerful means for helping you with your grief. However, I acknowledge not everyone is comfortable with journaling. If this is true for you, my experience suggests that simply taking the time to reflect on the questions can give new insights and be effective.

I do need to acknowledge that this book is about you, the suicide loss survivor, rather than about those who died by suicide. This is not a book about the "whys" of suicide. While I will explore the instinctive need to ask "why?" as part of the journey, I do not review the various explanations or motivations for suicide. Actually, detailed investigations of the factors that can lead to suicide demonstrate that there are many reasons people take their own lives. Suicide often has multiple determinates. That is, it is the result of a number of factors coming together. Often, these determinations may be masked or unknown to family members and friends. In fact, they may not even be visible to the person who ended his or her own life.

Finally, I want to acknowledge that this book may be difficult for you to read and process. As you read the touchstones that follow, allow yourself the time you need to fully engage with the words and the meaning. Reading too much in one sitting may be overwhelming. If this is the case for you, allow yourself to read short passages then set the book aside to come back to later. If you encounter discussion that seems too painful to explore right now, skip over those passages. Just as you need to dose yourself with your grief (see page 29), you may also need to dose yourself with the content of this book. And if and when this book stirs painful and difficult feelings within you, find a compassionate, nonjudgmental friend or grief-informed counselor to share them with.

EXPRESS YOURSELF:
Go to *The Understanding Your Suicide Grief Journal* on p. 16.

Reach Out to Your Fellow Survivors

I cannot emphasize enough how in my experience it is in the companionship of our fellow suicide loss survivors that we often find solace and support. As survivors we know not to judge each other. As survivors we share the same language. As survivors we can acknowledge our grief openly and without shame. As survivors we can honor our need to mourn in ways that are not based on speculation or gossip. As survivors we can go on to live and love fully until we die!

STAYING AWARE OF ACTIVATING EXPERIENCES

You are probably aware that certain things can make your grief ramp up from zero to 60 in a split second. Your grief and the grief of fellow suicide loss survivors can get "activated" through experiences such as: when methods of suicide are shared, specific details of the death are explored, you visit places where suicide deaths have taken place, or media coverage of suicide death occurs.

While the goal is not to stifle or shut down the need to authentically mourn, it is important to be mindful of how and when these activating experiences can naturally impact you and those around you. It is instinctive to want to avoid placing yourself in the path of these kind of activating experiences. Yet, encountering these activators can and will occur. So, when they do impact you, it is ok to do whatever you need to do to feel safe and comforted as much as possible.

It can also be helpful to have someone you trust debrief any activating experiences you encounter. As I often say, "grief shared is grief that can be softened slowly over time with no rewards for speed!"

Believe in Your Capacity to Heal

Yes, your life has been turned upside down by this suicide. You are faced with re-creating yourself as you search for the "new you." You are not the same person you were before the suicide. Your "divine spark"—that which gives your life meaning and purpose—has been muted. Yet, all of the suicide loss survivors I have had the privilege of meeting and learning from want me to tell you this: you will survive. You may think you cannot get through this, but you can and you will. Yes, you need to have the intention to sit in the wound, but over time and with the love and support of others, your grief will soften and you will find ways to be happy again. As you do your hard work of mourning, you can and will choose not to simply survive, but to truly live.

In Gratitude

I thank you for taking the time to read and reflect on the words that make up this book. It is people just like you who have been my teachers. I am also grateful to the thousands of people who have participated in my retreat learning experiences about grief and who have embraced the companioning philosophy I hold so dear. Most important, I thank those who have gone before me for teaching me that grief is a birthright of life and that giving and receiving love is the essence of having meaning and purpose in our lives.

I hope we meet one day.

Alan D. Wolfelt

TOUCHSTONE ONE

Open to the Presence of Your Loss

Someone you love has died by suicide. In your heart, you have come to know deep pain and suffering. To be "bereaved" literally means "to be torn apart." You have a broken heart and your life has been turned upside down.

From my own experience with the death of a close friend to suicide, as well as my experience of supporting thousands of suicide loss survivors over the years, I have learned that we cannot go around the pain that is the wilderness of grief. Instead, we must journey all through it, sometimes shuffling along the less strenuous side paths, sometimes plowing directly into the center.

> *"There is no greater agony than bearing an untold story inside you."*
>
> Maya Angelou

While it is instinctive to want to run as far away as possible from the overwhelming pain that comes with this loss, you have probably already discovered that even if you try to hide, deny, or self-treat your pain, it is still within you, demanding your attention. In acknowledging the inevitability of the pain and raw suffering that comes with this grief, in coming to understand the need to gently embrace the pain, you in effect honor the pain. "What?" you may naturally protest. "Honor the pain?"

Yes, as strange as it might sound, your pain is the key that opens your heart and ushers you on your way to eventual healing.

In many ways, the purpose of this book is to help you honor your pain. Honoring means recognizing the value of and respecting. I understand it is not instinctive to see grief that erupts following a suicide death and the need to mourn as something to honor. I certainly didn't want to honor my pain when my friend Ken took his life. However, I discovered that it was necessary and ultimately healing. I hope you discover as I did that to honor (value it, respect it, give it the attention it demands) your grief is not self-destructive or harmful, it is self-sustaining and life-giving.

WHAT IS HEALING IN GRIEF?

To heal in grief is to become whole again, to integrate your grief into yourself, and to learn to continue your changed life with fullness and meaning. Experiencing a new and changed "wholeness" requires that you engage in the work of mourning. It doesn't happen to you; you must stay open to that which has broken you.

Healing is a holistic concept that embraces the physical, cognitive, emotional, social, and spiritual areas of life. Note that healing is not the same as curing, which is a medical term that means "remedying" or "correcting." You cannot correct your grief, but you can heal your grief.

You have probably been taught that pain is an indication that something is wrong and that you should find a way to alleviate the pain. In our culture, pain and feelings of loss are experiences most people try to avoid. Why? Because the role of pain and suffering is misunderstood. This is particularly true with suicide grief. Because of the stigma and taboo surrounding suicide, many people think you should not talk about it, let alone honor your pain by openly and authentically mourning. Normal thoughts and feelings after a suicide death are still seen by some as unnecessary, even inappropriate.

You will learn over time, if you haven't already, that the pain of suicide grief will keep trying to get your attention until you have the courage to gently, and in small doses, open to its presence. The alternatives—denying, suppressing, or self-treating your pain—are in fact more painful.

I have learned that the pain that surrounds the closed heart of grief is the pain of living against yourself, the pain of denying how the loss changed you, the pain of feeling alone and

isolated—unable to openly mourn, unable to love and be loved by those around you. Denied grief results in what I term "living in the shadow of the ghosts of grief" (see my book by this title for an outline of the potential consequences of carrying your pain), which is a state in which you essentially risk dying while you are alive.

Instead of dying while you are alive, you can choose to allow yourself to remain open to the pain. Paradoxically, it is gathering courage to move toward the pain that ultimately leads to the healing of your wounded heart. Your integrity is engaged by your feelings and the commitment you make to honor the truth in them.

Taboo: Something society decides is so terrible that no one may be allowed to do it, talk about it, or learn about it.

Stigma: The mark of shame and ridicule placed on those people who die by suicide, and on their families. The stigma is the punishment for breaking the taboo.

People are often anxious and afraid of what they do not understand, so this stigma exists because of fear. So, sad to say, you may have to reach out and find safe, nonjudgmental people who support your need to mourn openly and honestly.

In part, this book will encourage you to be present to your multitude of thoughts and feelings, to "be with" them, for they contain the truth you are searching for, the energy you may be lacking, and the unfolding of your eventual healing. While it can be tempting to only want to allow a limited range of feelings to surface, my experience suggests you will need all of your thoughts and feelings to lead you there, not just the feelings you find acceptable. For it is in being honest with yourself that you find your way through the wilderness and identify the places that need to be healed.

EXPRESS YOURSELF:
Go to *The Understanding Your Suicide Grief Journal* on p. 18.

Staying Present to Your Pain

As you stay present to your pain that comes with the experience of suicide loss, you will be participating in "soul work," which will eventually lead to "spirit work". Keep in mind that "soul work" precedes "spirit work."

Soul Work: A downward movement in the psyche; a willingness to connect with what is dark, deep, and not pleasant.

Spirit Work: An upward movement in the psyche; embracing hope; and the relighting of one's divine spark.

In part, healing and the integration of grief are about your willingness to descend into your soul work on the path to your spirit work. My personal and professional experience suggests that when we experience the death of someone we care deeply about to suicide, we must allow ourselves to descend before we integrate the loss into our lives.

EXPRESS YOURSELF:
Go to *The Understanding Your Suicide Grief Journal* on p. 19.

DOSING YOUR PAIN

While this touchstone seeks to help you understand the role of pain in your healing, it is important to understand that you cannot embrace the pain of your grief in one sitting. If you were to feel it all at once, you could not survive. In fact, you could put yourself at risk for dying of a broken heart.

Instead, **you must invite yourself to "dose" your pain—to feel it in small waves then allow it to retreat until you're ready for the next wave.** In other words, I encourage you to remember to embrace your pain a little bit at a time, then set it aside and give yourself a break, allowing time for you to restore yourself and rebuild your energy to attend to your grief again.

(Continued on next page.)

For example, you might intentionally dose yourself with your pain for a few minutes or an hour once or twice each day in the coming weeks, then intentionally engage yourself in another activity that you find relaxing, pleasurable, distracting, or immersive.

I also call this back-and-forth of grief and respite "encounter—evade." You intentionally encounter your grief for a while, then you evade it until you're ready to encounter again.

Of course, you won't be able to completely escape your pain; even when you're not giving it your full attention. It will always be there, in the background, and it may forcefully break through to your other activities at any time. (I call this a "griefburst" and we'll talk more about it on p. 165.) But you cannot and shouldn't expect yourself to give the pain of your grief your full attention all the time. Befriending pain is fatiguing, difficult work, so it's absolutely essential to replenish your energy as often and as fully as you can.

Setting Your Intention to Heal

You are on a journey that is naturally frightening, painful, and often lonely. No words, written or spoken, can take away the pain you feel now. I hope, however, that this book will bring you some comfort and encouragement as you make a commitment to embracing that very pain.

It takes a true commitment to heal your grief. Yes, you are changed, but with commitment and intention you can and will become whole again. Commitment goes hand-in-hand with the concept of "setting your intention." Intention is defined as being conscious of what you want to experience. A close cousin to "affirmation," it is using the power of positive, focused thought to produce a desired result.

How can you use the power of intention in your journey through grief? By setting your intention to heal.

When you set your intention to heal, you make a true commitment to positively influence the course of your journey.

You choose between being what I call a "passive witness" or an "active participant" in your grief. I'm sure you have heard this tired cliché: Time heals all wounds. Yet time alone has little to do with healing. To heal, you must be willing to learn about the mystery of the grief journey. It can't be fixed or "resolved;" it can only be soothed and integrated through actively engaging with and expressing your many thoughts and feelings.

EXPRESS YOURSELF:
Go to *The Understanding Your Suicide Grief Journal* on pp. 20-21.

SPIRITUAL PESSIMISM VERSUS SPIRITUAL OPTIMISM

In grief, you can choose to be a spiritual pessimist or optimist. I recommend the latter.

What I mean by this is that it's up to you to decide how you will imagine your future and the beliefs that will guide you there.

For example, I have known grievers who have felt that if and when they experienced joy, they were somehow being disloyal to the person who died. This is a spiritually pessimistic belief, and it is one they are choosing, whether they know it or not. Spiritual optimists, conversely, opt to believe that they can continue to mourn and love the person who died while at the same time striving to live the remainder of their own precious days with purpose and joy.

My suggestion would be to purposefully and regularly set your intention to be a spiritual optimist!

Making Grief Your Friend

The concept of intention-setting presupposes that your outer reality is a direct reflection of your inner thoughts and beliefs. If you can change or mold some of your thoughts or beliefs, then you can influence your reality. In journaling and speaking (and potentially praying) your intentions, you can help set them.

You might tell yourself, "I can and will reach out for support during this difficult time in my life. I can and will find people who do not change the subject or feel a need to run away when I tell my story. I will look to people who can accept the new person I have become. I will become filled with hope that I can and will survive this death."

A SURVIVOR SPEAKS

"Once I decided I wanted to go on living, I committed myself to facing what I had to face. It's been so hard, but it has been more than worth it."

Setting your intention like the above example is not only a way of helping yourself heal (although it is indeed that!), but also a way of actively guiding your grief. Of course, you will still have to honor and embrace your pain during this time. By honoring the presence of your pain, by understanding the appropriateness of your pain, you are committing to facing the pain. You are committing to pay attention to your experience in ways that allow you to eventually begin to breathe life into your soul again. What better reason to give attention to your intention!

INTEGRATION OR RECONCILIATION

An important concept to keep in mind as you journey through grief is that of *integration* or *reconciliation*. You cannot get over or resolve your grief, but you can integrate or reconcile yourself to it. That is, you can learn to incorporate your grief into your consciousness and re-discover meaning and purpose in your life. See Touchstone Nine for more on integration and reconciliation.

In reality, denying your grief, running from it, or minimizing it often only makes it more confusing and overwhelming. Paradoxically, to eventually soften your heart, you must embrace your grief. As strange as it may seem, you must make it your friend.

In this book, I will attempt to teach you to gently and lovingly befriend your grief. To not be ashamed to express it. To not be ashamed of your tears and profound feelings of sadness. To not pull down the blinds that shut out light and love. Slowly and in doses, you can and will return to life and begin to live in ways that put stars back into your sky.

EXPRESS YOURSELF:
Go to *The Understanding Your Suicide Grief Journal* on p. 22.

No Reward for Speed

Reconciling your grief does not happen quickly or efficiently. The grief work surrounding suicide may be some of the hardest work you ever do. Because grief is work, it naturally leaves you feeling drained. That is why you probably are experiencing what is called "lethargy of grief," where you don't feel like you have any physical, emotional, or spiritual energy.

Consequently, you must be patient with yourself. When you come to trust the pain will not last forever, it becomes tolerable. **Deceiving yourself into thinking the pain does not even exist is sure to make it intolerable.** Spiritual maturity in your grief work is attained when you embrace a paradox: to live at once in the state of both encounter and surrender, to both "work at" and "surrender to" your grief.

As you come to know this paradox, you will slowly discover the soothing of your soul. Resist the need to figure out everything with your head, and let the paradox embrace you. You will find yourself wrapped in a gentle peace—the peace of living at once in both *encounter* (feeling the pain of your grief) and *surrender* (embracing the mystery without trying to "understand" it with your head).

EXPRESS YOURSELF:
Go to *The Understanding Your Suicide Grief Journal* on p. 22.

A Vital Distinction: Shock Versus Denial

Shock along with elements of denial is a temporary, healthy response that essentially says, "The reality of the suicide death of someone in my life is too painful to acknowledge right now. Therefore, I refuse to believe it." **While this is a natural initial reaction to suicide, you will hinder your eventual healing if you stay in long-term denial.**

There are various forms of denial that as a survivor, you must work to break through:

Conscious Denial: This is where you hide the fact that the death was suicide. You may tell people it was a heart attack, homicide, or an unexplained sudden death.

Innocent Denial: This is where you hold onto the hope that the findings that ruled the death a suicide were a mistake and will be changed at a later date.

A SURVIVOR SPEAKS

"At first, I couldn't even get my feet out of the bed. It was a major accomplishment to take a shower. I would say with my head, 'Get going,' but my body said, 'You aren't going anywhere.'"

Blame as Denial: This is where you blame someone else for the suicide, thereby denying the choice someone made to take his or her own life.

Pretense and Denial: This is where the family rule is that you never talk about the death or use the word suicide at any time.

The various motivations for these forms of denial are often multiple and complex. Often, people don't even realize they are in denial. So, if you discover you have gone beyond shock into some form of prolonged denial, do not shame or ridicule yourself.

But here is the problem: By staying in whatever form of denial, you miss the opportunity to do the grief work related to your feelings. You inhibit your capacity to experience perturbation (see page 13). As you have seen emphasized in this touchstone, befriending your pain is central to your ultimate healing. Until denial is broken through and the pain is experienced, you are on hold and authentic mourning cannot take place.

If you find yourself stuck in denial, commit yourself to working on this first and foremost. There is good reason that I address this in Touchstone One of this book. Why? Because until you break through any form of denial, the additional touchstones that follow do you little good. Of course, if you were in long-term denial you probably would not be reading this book. Perhaps you know some family members and friends who will not read this book, preferring to maintain their personal denial.

A SURVIVOR SPEAKS

"I went from shock into denial and stayed there for a long time. Ultimately, I discovered I was becoming my own worst enemy. Fortunately, I found a compassionate counselor who gently led the way and invited me to face the reality of the suicide of my son. That is when my mourning really started."

EXPRESS YOURSELF:
Go to *The Understanding Your Suicide Grief Journal* on p. 23.

A SPECIAL CAUTION

You may have some people in your family or friendship system who totally refuse to acknowledge that the cause of death was suicide. You must overcome any instinct to think your role is to convince them that the death was a suicide. Forcing them to confront the facts is often perceived as insensitive and inappropriate. Some people stay in denial for long periods of time, some even until their own death. Be patient and kind. You are responsible *to* people, not *for* them. What I as a therapist might do to help someone gently confront the reality of suicide is very different than you confronting a family member or friend.

Face Any Inappropriate Expectations

Through no fault of your own, you are at risk for having inappropriate expectations surrounding this death. These expectations result from common societal messages that tell you to "be strong" in the face of life losses. Invariably, some well-intentioned people around you will urge you to "move on," "let go," "keep your chin up," and "keep busy". Actually, you need to give yourself as much time as you need to mourn, and these kinds of comments hurt you, not help you.

Often combined with these messages is an unstated but strong belief that you have a right not to hurt, so do whatever you can to avoid it. The unfortunate result is that you may be encouraged by some people to be happy despite the pain of your loss, self-treat your pain in some way, or try to deny your profound feelings of grief.

Society often tends to make us feel shame or embarrassment about our feelings of grief, particularly suicide grief. Shame can be described as the feeling that something you are doing is bad. And you may feel that if you mourn, then you should be ashamed. If you are perceived as "doing well," you are often seen as "being strong" and "under control." The message is that the well-controlled person stays rational at all times. (See more on embarrassment on p. 110.)

Combined with this message is another one. Society erroneously implies that if you, as a grieving person, openly express your feelings of grief, you are being immature. If your feelings are fairly intense, you may be labeled overly emotional or needy. If your feelings are extremely intense and long-lasting, you may even be referred to as "crazy" or as having "Prolonged Grief Disorder."

As a professional grief counselor, I assure you that you are not immature, overly emotional, or "crazy." I often say that society has it backwards in defining who is "doing well" in grief and who is "not doing well."

From an early age, you may have been taught to conceal emotions, particularly emotions like sadness, anxiety, and depression. You may have learned to put on a happy face and to have a stiff upper lip. Perhaps you were even exposed to the saying, "Laugh and the world laughs with you; weep and you weep alone."

If you fear emotions and see them as negative, you will be at risk for grieving alone and in isolation. You will be at risk for trying to run from and hide from some very real human emotions that try to surface when someone you care about dies by suicide. Of course, shame and secrecy then continue.

Yet, being secretive with your emotions does not integrate your painful feelings of loss; it complicates them. Then even more pain comes from trying to keep the pain secret. You cannot hide your feelings *and* find renewed meaning in your life. If you are dishonest about your pain, you stay in pain.

Being dishonest with your emotions surrounding this suicide death may temporarily help you get through each day, but it will catch up with you in the end. In essence, you can mourn now or mourn later. In reality, the pain of grief is so powerful it will eventually catch up to you. Healing is a process of truth, and you cannot experience truth if you are dishonest with your emotions. **If you deny the emotions of your heart, you deny the essence of your life.**

To be open to the presence of your loss, you must accept that you are not wrong to feel what you feel, be it anger, sadness, guilt, fear, or any other emotion. There is no such thing as a negative emotion. If you judge yourself for mourning, you will feel shame. When it comes to healing the wounds of suicide grief, honesty is the best policy.

When you open to the presence of your loss, you will see that no feeling is inherently bad, negative, or wrong. By being honest with yourself and others, the pain you feel begins to soften. It is through being honest that you discover you are not alone and that compassionate people are available to be supportive to you.

EXPRESS YOURSELF:
Go to *The Understanding Your Suicide Grief Journal* on p. 23.

Grief is Not a Disease

You have probably already discovered that no quick fix exists for the pain you are enduring. Grief following a suicide is naturally complex, and it is easy to feel overwhelmed. But I promise you that if you can think, feel, and see yourself as an active participant in your healing, you will slowly but surely experience a renewed sense of meaning and purpose in your life.

Grief is not a disease; it is a normal part of love. To be human means coming to know loss as part of your life. Many losses, or "little griefs," occur along life's path. And not all of your losses are as painful as others; they do not always disconnect you from yourself. But the suicide death of someone you have cared deeply about is likely to leave you feeling disconnected from both yourself and the outside world.

Yet, while grief is a powerful experience, so, too, is your capacity to aid your own healing. In your willingness to: 1) read and reflect on the pages in this book; 2) complete the companion journal, at your own pace; and 3) possibly participate in a support group with fellow suicide loss survivors, you are demonstrating your commitment and setting your intention to reinvest in life while never forgetting the person who died.

I invite you to gently and in doses confront and befriend the pain of your grief. I will try with all my heart to show you how to look for the touchstones on your journey through the wilderness of grief so that your life can proceed with meaning and purpose.

EXPRESS YOURSELF:
Go to *The Understanding Your Suicide Grief Journal* on p. 24.

A SURVIVOR SPEAKS

"At first I thought my feelings meant I was being weak. So I tried to stay strong. But in a support group I learned that my feelings were not out to get me! They were actually trying to tell me to give attention to my need to openly, and without any sense of shame, mourn. Now I have learned to have gratitude for my ability to feel."

Attention, Compassion, and Expression

This touchstone is one of the most difficult for many grieving people to surrender to. The concept of the need to not just acknowledge but attend to and even befriend your pain is something you may find yourself naturally resisting. Yet allow me to remind you that the pain of your loss is both normal and necessary. It is a natural human response, and more than that, it is productive pain. Your pain exists to ask for your attention, compassion, and expression because these are the very approaches that will allow you to integrate your grief over time and eventually heal. Besides, without the pain of grief, there would be no such thing as the joy of love.

Our culture's belief that pain is something to be avoided or immediately "fixed" is a pervasive grief misconception. We'll be exploring such misconceptions in the next touchstone. Then, once we've cleared away much of the debris blocking your path into the wilderness of authentic grief and healing, we will be able to move on to deeper truths about your unique journey.

Dispel Misconceptions About Grief

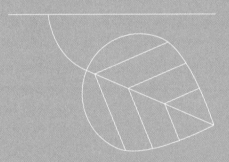

> **MISCONCEPTION**
>
> A misconception is a mistaken notion you might have about something—in other words, something you believe to be true but that is not true. Misconceptions about grief are common in our society because we tend not to openly mourn or talk about grief and mourning. You can see how we would have misconceptions about something surrounded in taboo and stigma as is suicide grief.

As you journey through the wilderness of your suicide grief, if you mourn openly and authentically, you will come to find a path that feels right for you. That is your path to healing. But beware—others may try to pull you off this path. They may try to make you believe that the path you have chosen is wrong and that their way is better.

The reason that people try to pull you from the path is that they have often internalized some common misconceptions about suicide grief and mourning. As a result, this may make you doubt or judge yourself unfairly. **The misconceptions, in essence, deny you your right to hurt and authentically express your grief. They often cause unrealistic expectations about the grief experience.** To integrate this loss into your soul, you must first be willing to unlearn the following misconceptions.

"We have to find ways to unlearn those things that screen us from the perception of profound truth."

Thomas Moore

As you read about this important touchstone, you may discover that you yourself have believed in some of the misconceptions and that some may be embraced by people around you. Don't condemn yourself or others for believing in them if this is the case. They can seem like common sense, and it is also easy to believe something about which you have no actual experience. Simply make use of any new insights you might gain to help you open your heart to your work of mourning in ways that restore your soul.

MISCONCEPTION 1:

Grief and mourning are the same thing.

Perhaps you have noticed that people tend to use the words "grieving" and "mourning" interchangeably. However, there is an important distinction.

Grief is the constellation of internal thoughts and feelings we have when someone we are attached to dies. Think of grief as the container. It holds all of your thoughts, feelings, and images of your experience when you are bereaved. In other words, grief is the internal meaning given to the experience of loss.

Bereavement: "to be torn apart," "to have unique needs," "to be robbed."

Mourning, on the other hand, is when we take our inner grief and express it outside of ourselves in some way. Another way of defining mourning is "grief gone public" or "the outward expression of grief." Talking about the person who died, crying, expressing your thoughts and feelings through art or music, and celebrating special anniversary dates that held meaning for the person who died are just a few examples of mourning.

Grief comes naturally, but mourning usually takes intentional effort and commitment. It's worth it, though, because the only way to move toward fully integrating loss into our lives and eventually healing is not just by grieving but by mourning.

Mourning is active. Mourning is work. You will move toward reconciliation (see p. 222) not just by grieving but through deliberate, ongoing mourning.

A major theme of this book is rooted in the importance of openly and honestly mourning the suicide death, in expressing your grief outside of yourself. Over time and with the support of others, to mourn is to heal.

WARNING: After someone you love has died by suicide, some of your family and friends may encourage you to keep your grief to yourself. If you were to take this message to heart, the disastrous result would be that all of your thoughts and feelings would stay neatly bottled up inside you. A catalyst for healing, however, can only be created when you develop the courage to mourn publicly, in the presence of understanding, compassionate people who will not judge you. At times, of course, you will grieve alone, but expressing your grief outside of yourself is necessary if you are to slowly and eventually move forward in your grief.

I think it's so interesting that many native cultures actually create vessels, usually baskets, pots, or bowls, that symbolically contain their grief. They put these vessels away for periods of time, only to bring them out on a regular basis to help themselves mourn.

Another way to think about what these cultures are instinctively doing is dosing themselves with their grief. As I've said, grief must be embraced little by little, in small bits, with breaks in between. This dosing helps you survive what, if absorbed in its totality all at once, would probably overwhelm you.

When you don't honor a death loss by acknowledging it, first to yourself and then to those around you, the grief will accumulate. Then the denied loss comes flowing out in all sorts of potential ways (e.g., anxiety, depression, physical complaints, difficulty in relationships, addictive behaviors), compounding your loss.

EXPRESS YOURSELF:
Go to *The Understanding Your Suicide Grief Journal* on pp. 26-27.

MISCONCEPTION 2:

Grief following a suicide death always results in "Complicated Mourning" or "Prolonged Grief Disorder."

Actually, there is research that indicates that suicide loss survivors integrate grief at about the same pace as those who experience any kind of unanticipated death. This misconception could have you believing that you should suffer longer.

This does not mean that a suicide death won't be viewed differently (see the circumstances of death, p. 64). Obviously, there can be some natural challenges, such as the combination of sudden shock, the natural question of "why?", the trauma of witnessing or discovering the suicide, the lack of support from family and friends, and the potential of "secondary victimization" that results from cruel, judgmental, or insensitive comments. Yes, you will have griefbursts (see p. 165) and naturally do some "catch-up" mourning as you continue with your life, but do not let this misconception become a self-fulfilling prophecy. So, while there can be a natural risk for complications in your grief, don't let anyone project onto you that you will definitely experience what some call "Prolonged Grief Disorder." Do your work of mourning, and you will come out of the dark and into the light.

EXPRESS YOURSELF:
Go to *The Understanding Your Suicide Grief Journal* on p. 28.

MISCONCEPTION 3:

Grief and mourning progress in predictable, orderly stages.

You have probably heard of the "stages of grief." This type of thinking about dying, grief, and mourning is appealing but inaccurate. The notion of stages helps people make sense of death, an experience that is usually not orderly or predictable. If we believe that everyone grieves by going through the same stages, then death and grief become much less mysterious and fearsome. If only it were so simple!

The concept of grief stages was popularized in 1969 with the publication of Elisabeth Kübler-Ross's landmark text *On Death and Dying.* In this groundbreaking book, Kübler-Ross listed the five stages of grief that she saw terminally ill patients experience in the face of their own impending deaths: denial; anger; bargaining; depression; and acceptance. However, Kübler-Ross never intended for her stages to be interpreted as a rigid, linear sequence to be followed by all grieving people. However, our culture has done just that, and the consequences have often been disastrous.

As a grieving person, you will probably encounter others who have adopted a rigid system of beliefs about what you should and shouldn't experience in your grief journey—whether they adhere to the Kübler-Ross stages or an understanding wholly their own. And if you have internalized this misconception, you may also find yourself trying to prescribe and dictate your own grief experience as well. Instead of allowing yourself to be where you are on any given day, you may shame yourself or try to force yourself to be in a certain "stage."

For example, you may or may not experience normal grief symptoms of disorganization, fear, guilt, and explosive emotions (all of which we'll talk about in Touchstone Four) during your unique grief journey. Or you might move through one or more of these feelings, think you're "done" with it, then find yourself returning to it later on. Sometimes you may move from one predominant emotion to another in a short period of time. At other times, and perhaps more commonly, you may experience two or more emotions simultaneously.

Remember—do not try to determine where you "should" be in your grief. Just allow yourself to be naturally where you are and

present to whatever you're experiencing in each moment.

Everyone mourns in different ways. Personal experience is your best teacher about where you are in your grief journey. Don't think your goal is to move through prescribed stages. As you read further in this book, you will find that a major theme is understanding that your grief is unique. The word unique means "only one." No one ever existed exactly like you before, and no one will ever be exactly like you again. As part of the healing process, the thoughts and feelings you will experience will be totally unique to you.

EXPRESS YOURSELF:
Go to *The Understanding Your Suicide Grief Journal* on pp. 28-29.

MISCONCEPTION 4:

We can always determine the "whys?" of a suicide death.

You may naturally have some of what I like to refer to as psycho-spiritual "why?" questions. You may search for answers, look for clues, and try to make sense of the "why?" of this person's death. Do not punish yourself for this instinctive response. Why did the person do this can be a painful yet natural question to explore. As a matter of fact, watch out for well-intentioned people who say, "Don't ask why; it doesn't do you any good." Those people often do not understand the normalcy of how "why?" questions precede "how?" questions. "Why did this happen?" is part of the pathway to get yourself to "How will I survive that he or she did this?" Again, do not shame yourself if you find this is part of your experience.

Having acknowledged the normalcy of "why?" questions, detailed investigation of the factors that can lead to a suicide death demonstrate that there are usually many reasons people take their own lives. There is no way to prevent what you cannot predict. Suicide is rarely the result of just one person, a single conversation, or one event. Specific reasons may be unknown or masked to family members and friends. In fact, they are often not even able to be seen by the person who died by suicide.

So, the misconception is that we always know why, when the reality is we often don't know the specifics of why. My experience with many survivors suggests that you may very slowly, with no rewards for speed, discover that it is possible to live with the uncertainty of never fully knowing the answer to "why?"

EXPRESS YOURSELF:
Go to *The Understanding Your Suicide Grief Journal* on p. 30.

MISCONCEPTION 5:
All suicide loss survivors feel guilty.

The sad reality is that some people may actually say directly to you, "I bet you feel guilty" or pose the question, "Do you feel guilty?" This is one of the most prescribed responses for suicide loss survivors. Many books about suicide survivorship give the most coverage to the topic of guilt.

In reality, as a survivor you may or may not feel guilty. Besides, assuming you feel guilt is the opposite of my belief that you are the expert of your own experience and therefore you must teach me what you feel; I must not prescribe what you should feel.

People do not know how you feel unless they give you the opportunity to teach them. People do not automatically assume survivors feel guilty after a death from a heart attack or cancer. Therefore, we should not assume guilt after a suicide death. Many survivors have worked long and hard to try to help someone prior to a suicide death.

As one astute person noted, "This assumption, from the Dark Ages, that we should have some brand to show people our guilt and shame from having a suicide in the family lives on." So, if you are experiencing guilt, find a safe place with caring people where you can explore it. But I encourage you – do not assume you have to feel guilty.

EXPRESS YOURSELF:
Go to *The Understanding Your Suicide Grief Journal* on pp. 31-32.

MISCONCEPTION 6:
Only certain kinds of people die by suicide.

This is a simple misconception to dispel. The reality is that suicide is a stranger to no race, creed, religion, age group, sexual orientation, gender identification, income bracket, or socioeconomic level. All kinds of people have died by suicide since the beginning of recorded history.

EXPRESS YOURSELF:
Go to *The Understanding Your Suicide Grief Journal* on p. 32.

MISCONCEPTION 7:
Only a "crazy" person dies by suicide.

While the person who died by suicide may have been depressed, anxious, or hopeless, most of us survivors don't find comfort when people try to tell us the person was "crazy". Not all suicides meet some formal criteria for mental health diagnosis, and even when they do, we don't need to hear that they were "crazy."

Related to this, according to the American Association of Suicidology (AAS), approximately two-thirds of people who die by suicide are depressed, and the risk of suicide in people with major depression is about twenty times that of the general population. Depression, often undiagnosed and untreated, is the major cause of suicide.

Again, some people will think they are helping you when they claim your loved one must have been "crazy". However, this does not lighten your burden and uplift your spirit. And, it is not a good use of language to assist in your understanding. **Even when the person you cared about so deeply had a diagnosable mental health challenge, we don't need to use the word crazy.** For more on the use of the word "crazy," see page 153.

EXPRESS YOURSELF:
Go to *The Understanding Your Suicide Grief Journal* on p. 33.

MISCONCEPTION 8:

It is a sin to die by suicide, and the person who does goes directly to hell.

It was not all that long ago that suicide was considered a sin by many of the major bodies of faith. Historically, it was considered by many not just a sin, but an unpardonable sin.

Fortunately, we now have religious leaders and well-respected theologians who are compassionately and non-judgmentally educating people that suicide is not a sin. As one Catholic priest observed about suicide, "When its victims wake on the other side, they are met by a gentle Christ who stands right inside of their huddled fear and says, 'Peace be with you!' As we see in the gospels, God can go through locked doors, breathe out peace in places where we cannot get in, and write straight with even the most crooked of lines."

But watch out for some people who do continue to preach this. Find people who recognize that faith is about being open to the mystery. I always like to remind myself that "mystery"—the ancient name for God—is something to be pondered, not explained. **If someone starts preaching to you that suicide is a sin and that your loved one has gone to hell, it is appropriate to set boundaries with them.**

Personally, I believe there are no limits to God's compassion. God mourns with us and doesn't send our loved ones to "burn in hell" as someone might try to tell you. If you believe as I do that God's nature is one of steadfast mercy and love, then we realize this is a misconception we need to keep educating the world about.

EXPRESS YOURSELF:
Go to *The Understanding Your Suicide Grief Journal* on p. 33.

MISCONCEPTION 9:
Suicide is inherited and runs in the family.

Be alert for uninformed people who may project to you that because someone in your family died by suicide, you may have the same fate. This projection is not supported by the facts. Scientific research has not at this time confirmed a genetic basis for suicide risk. Please do not listen to people who try to tell you are doomed to one day die by suicide.

Having acknowledged the obvious, we do know through research that substance abuse disorders, depressive disorders, and schizophrenia tend to run in families. However, even if you have family members who have died by suicide after having suffered from these types of mental health diagnoses, you are not predestined to die by suicide. So, again, do not let anyone tell you that you are.

Instead, if you are just being wise and self-compassionate, you will use this research information to do what you can to reduce your risk. This can include educating yourself about the warning signs related to risk for suicide, not abusing alcohol or drugs, and not hesitating to seek help whenever you may need it.

EXPRESS YOURSELF:
Go to *The Understanding Your Suicide Grief Journal* on p. 34.

MISCONCEPTION 10:
You should move away from suicide grief, not toward it.

Our society often encourages prematurely moving away from grief instead of toward it. The result is that too many mourners either grieve in isolation or attempt to deny, suppress, or run away from their grief through various means.

During ancient times, Stoic philosophers encouraged their followers not to mourn, believing that self-control was the appropriate response to sorrow. Today you may find that some well-intentioned but uninformed family and friends still adhere to this long-held tradition. While the outward expression of grief is a requirement for healing, overcoming society's powerful message to repress and deny can be difficult.

As a grief counselor, I'm often asked, "How long should grief last?" This question itself is an outgrowth of our cultural impatience with grief and the desire to move people away from pain and suffering. Just a few weeks after a death, grievers are often expected to be "back to normal."

Mourners who continue to express their grief outwardly, on the other hand, are often viewed as "weak," "crazy," or "self-pitying." The subtle message is, "Suck it up and get on with your life." The disturbing result is that far too many people view grief as something to be overcome rather than experienced.

These messages, unfortunately, encourage you to repress your normal and necessary thoughts and feelings about the death of someone loved. You may find yourself refusing to cry, for example, because suffering in silence and "being strong" are considered admirable. Many people have internalized society's misconception that mourning should be done quietly, quickly, and efficiently. My hope is this doesn't happen to you.

After the death of someone loved, you also may feel pressured to respond to the polite question, "How are you?" with the benign response, "I'm fine." In essence, you are saying to the world, "I'm not mourning." Some friends, family, and coworkers may encourage this stance. Why? Because they have also internalized this misconception and don't want to think or talk about death. So if you are stoic and do not outwardly mourn, your behavior is often considered more socially acceptable.

However, this inhibiting collaborative pretense about mourning does not meet your needs in grief. When your grief is ignored or minimized, you'll feel further isolated in your journey. Ultimately, you may experience the onset of the "Am I going crazy?" syndrome (see Touchstone Six). Masking or moving away from your grief only creates anxiety, confusion, and depression. If you receive little or no social recognition of your normal, natural pain, you will probably begin to fear that your thoughts and feelings are abnormal.

Remember—society will often encourage you to prematurely move away from your grief. **Instead, you must continually remind yourself that only leaning toward the pain will give you the divine momentum you need to begin to reconcile your grief and heal.**

EXPRESS YOURSELF:
Go to *The Understanding Your Suicide Grief Journal* on pp. 35-36.

MISCONCEPTION 11:

Tears of grief are only a sign of weakness.

While tears of grief are often associated with personal inadequacy and weakness, the worst thing you can do is to allow this wrongheaded notion to prevent you from crying.

Some people who care about you may, directly or indirectly, try to prevent your tears out of a well-intentioned but misguided desire to protect you and them from pain. You may hear comments like, "Tears won't bring him back" or "He wouldn't want you to cry." Yet, for many people, crying is an instinctive, helpful act of mourning. It's nature's way of releasing internal tension and stress hormones from your body. What's more, it allows you to communicate a need to be comforted. So don't let others stifle your need to mourn openly, even if it makes those around you feel helpless.

Tears of grief foster genuine healing. In my experience companioning mourners, I have witnessed this transformation up close many times. Not only do people say they feel better after crying, but they also look better. Tension and agitation seem to flow out of their bodies. After a good cry, they feel a little looser and less burdened.

You must be vigilant about guarding yourself against this misconception. Tears are not a sign of weakness. In fact, your capacity to share tears is an indication of your willingness to do the essential healing work of mourning.

EXPRESS YOURSELF:
Go to *The Understanding Your Suicide Grief Journal* on pp. 36-37.

MISCONCEPTION 12:
Being upset and openly mourning means you are being "weak" in your faith.

Watch out for those who think that having faith and openly mourning are mutually exclusive. Sometimes people fail to remember those important words of wisdom: "Blessed are those who mourn, for they shall be comforted."

Above all, mourning is a spiritual journey of the heart and soul. If faith or spirituality is a part of your life, express it in ways that seem appropriate to you. If you are mad at God, be mad at God. Actually, being angry at God speaks of having a relationship with God in the first place. I've always said to myself and others, "God has been doing very well for some time now — so I think God can handle my anger." Grief expressed is often grief diminished.

Similarly, if you need a time-out from regular worship, don't shame yourself. Going to exile for a period of time often assists in your eventual healing. If people insist you attend a place of worship, let them know you appreciate their concern but that you will go only if and when you are ready.

In the meantime, I encourage you to tend to your spirit each day. Do whatever helps you feel present, peaceful, and one with creation. Spending a few minutes in nature is often a good way to do this. Prayer, meditation, yoga, journaling, and listening to music that is meaningful to you are other ways.

Don't let people take your grief away from you in the name of faith —but do take care of your spirit.

EXPRESS YOURSELF:
Go to *The Understanding Your Suicide Grief Journal* on p. 38.

MISCONCEPTION 13:
When someone you love dies by suicide, you only grieve and mourn for the physical loss of the person.

When someone you love dies by suicide, you don't just lose the presence of that person. As a result of the death, you may lose many other connections to yourself and the world around you. Sometimes I outline these potential losses, or what I call "ripple-effect losses," as follows:

LOSS OF SELF
- *self*
  "I feel like part of me died when he died."

- *identity*
  You may have to rethink your role as husband or wife, mother or father, son or daughter, best friend, etc.

- *self-confidence*
  Some grievers experience lowered self-esteem. Naturally, you may have lost one of the people in your life who gave you confidence.

- *health*
  Physical symptoms of mourning.

- *personality*
  "I just don't feel like myself…"

LOSS OF SECURITY
- *emotional security*
  An emotional source of support is now gone, causing emotional upheaval.

- *physical security*
  You may not feel as safe living in your home or community as you did before.

- *financial security*
  You may have new financial concerns or have to learn to manage finances in ways you didn't before.

- *lifestyle*
  Your lifestyle doesn't feel the same as it did before.

LOSS OF MEANING

- *goals and dreams*
  Hopes and dreams for the future can be shattered.

- *faith*
  You may question your faith or belief system.

- *will/desire to live*
  You may have questions related to future meaning in your life. You may ask, "Why go on...?"

- *joy*
  Life's most precious emotion, happiness, is naturally compromised by the death of someone we love.

Allowing yourself to acknowledge the many levels of loss the suicide death has brought to your life will help you continue to stay open to your unique grief journey.

EXPRESS YOURSELF:
Go to *The Understanding Your Suicide Grief Journal* on p. 39.

MISCONCEPTION 14:

You should try not to think about the person who died by suicide on special days like holidays, anniversaries, and birthdays.

As with all things in grief, trying not to think about something that your heart and soul are nudging you to think about is a bad idea.

SECONDARY VICTIMIZATION

This is when, in this time of great loss and vulnerability in your life, someone knowingly or unknowingly victimizes you further by shaming you, accusing you, or otherwise making you feel even worse about the death. For example, someone whose son had taken his own life was told by a friend whose child has also died, "Your child chose to die. Mine didn't." Comments like those are not only hurtful, they may compound your already complicated feelings of grief.

On special occasions such as holidays, anniversaries such as wedding dates and the day the person died, and your birthday or the birthday of the person who died, it's natural for your grief to well up inside of you and spill over—even long after the death itself.

It may seem logical that if you can only avoid thinking about the person who died on these special days—maybe you can cram your day so tight that you don't have a second to spare—then you can avoid some heartache. What I would ask you is this: **Where does that heartache go if you don't let it out when it naturally arises? It doesn't disappear. It simply bides its time, patiently at first, then urgently, like a caged animal pacing behind bars.**

No doubt you have some family and friends who may attempt to perpetuate this misconception. Actually, they are really trying to protect themselves in the name of protecting you.

While you may feel particularly sad, vulnerable, and lonely during these times, remember—these feelings are honest expressions of the real you. It's normal to feel your grief more deeply on special days. And it's good to find ways to be present to your feelings and to express them.

To give yourself the time and energy you need to befriend your grief on special days, I suggest not overextending yourself in other ways.

Don't feel you have to shop, bake, entertain, send cards, etc. if you're not feeling up to it.

Instead of avoiding these days, you may want to commemorate the life of the person who died by doing something he or she would have appreciated. On his birthday, what could you do to honor his special passions? On the anniversary of her death, what could you do to remember her life? You might want to spend these times in the company of people who help you feel safe and cared for and in whose company you can openly express your normal, necessary grief.

EXPRESS YOURSELF:
Go to *The Understanding Your Suicide Grief Journal* on pp. 40-41.

MISCONCEPTION 15:

After someone you love dies by suicide, the goal should be to "get over" your grief as soon as possible.

You may already have heard the question, "Are you over it yet?" Or, even worse, be told, "Well, you should be over it by now!" To think that as a human being you "get over" your grief is ludicrous! You don't get over it, you learn to live with it. You learn to integrate it into your life and into the fabric of your being. **As you become willing to do the work of your mourning, however, you can and will become reconciled to it.** Unfortunately, if the people around you expect you to "get over" your grief, they set you up to fail.

EXPRESS YOURSELF:
Go to *The Understanding Your Suicide Grief Journal* on pp. 42-43.

MISCONCEPTION 16:

Nobody can help you with your grief.

We have all heard people say, "Nobody can help you but yourself." Or you may have been told since childhood, "If you want something done right, do it yourself." **Yet, in reality, perhaps the most**

compassionate thing you can do for yourself at this difficult time is to reach out for help from others.

Think of it this way: Grieving and mourning may be the hardest work you have ever done. And hard work is less burdensome when others lend a hand. Life's greatest challenges – getting through school, raising children, and pursuing a career – are in many ways team efforts. So it should be with mourning.

Sharing your pain with others won't make it disappear, but it will, over time, make it more bearable. By definition, mourning (i.e., the outward expression of grief) requires that you get support from sources outside of yourself. Grieving may be a solo activity, but mourning is often not. Reaching out for help also connects you to other people and strengthens the bonds of love that make life seem worth living again.

EXPRESS YOURSELF:
Go to *The Understanding Your Suicide Grief Journal* on pp. 43-44.

MISCONCEPTION 17:

When grief and mourning are finally reconciled, they never come up again.

If only this were so. As your experience has probably already taught you, grief comes in and out like waves from the ocean. Sometimes when you least expect it, a huge wave comes along and pulls your feet right out from under you.

Sometimes heightened periods of sadness overwhelm us when we're in grief—even years after the death. These times can seem to come out of nowhere and can be frightening and painful. Something as simple as a sound, a smell, or phrase can bring on what I call "griefbursts." My friend Ken loved the Wisconsin Badgers football team. Every time I see something on TV about that team I have a griefburst.

Allow yourself to experience griefbursts without shame or self-

judgment, no matter where or when they occur. Sooner or later, one will probably happen when you're surrounded by other people, maybe even strangers. If you would feel more comfortable, retreat to somewhere more private, or go see someone you know who will understand, when these strong feelings surface. (For more on griefbursts, see p. 165.)

You will always, for the rest of your life, feel some grief over this death. It will no longer dominate your life, but it will always be there, in the background, reminding you about the attachment you had for the person who died.

EXPRESS YOURSELF:
Go to *The Understanding Your Suicide Grief Journal* on p. 45.

Keep in mind that the misconceptions about grief and mourning explored in this touchstone are certainly not all the misconceptions about suicide grief and mourning. Use the space provided in *The Understanding Your Suicide Grief Journal* (p. 46) to note any other grief misconceptions you have encountered since the suicide death of someone in your life.

When surrounded by people who believe these misconceptions, you will probably feel a heightened sense of isolation. If the people who are closest to you are unable to emotionally and spiritually support you without judging you, seek out others who can. Usually, the ability to be supportive without judging is most developed in people who have been on a grief journey themselves and are willing to be with you during this difficult time. When you are surrounded by people who can distinguish the misconceptions of grief from the realities, you can and will experience the healing you deserve.

Now that we've reviewed the common misconceptions of grief, let's wrap up Touchstone Two by listing some of the "conceptions." These are some realities you can hold onto as you journey toward healing.

Realistic Expectations for Grief and Mourning

- You will naturally grieve, but you will probably have to make a conscious effort to mourn.

- Your grief and mourning will involve a wide variety of different thoughts and feelings.

- Your grief and mourning will impact you in all five areas of experience: physical, cognitive, emotional, social, and spiritual.

- You need to feel it to heal it.

- Your grief will probably hurt more before it hurts less.

- Your grief will be unpredictable and will not likely progress in an orderly fashion.

- You don't "get over" grief; you learn to live with it.

- You need other people to help you through your grief.

- You will not always feel this bad.

Now that you've considered what might be realistic expectations for you to have about your journey through the wilderness of suicide grief, let's turn to a discussion of what makes your unique grief just that – unique.

EXPRESS YOURSELF:
Go to *The Understanding Your Suicide Grief Journal* on pp. 47-48.

TOUCHSTONE THREE

Embrace the
Uniqueness of Your Grief

The wilderness of your grief is your wilderness. The death of someone from suicide feels unlike any other loss you may have experienced. The traumatic nature of the death may leave you feeling turned inside out and upside down. Your wilderness may be rockier or more level than others. Your path may be revealed in a straight line, or, more likely, it may be full of twists and turns. In the wilderness of your journey, you will experience the topography in your own unique way.

> *"This moment, this day, this relationship, this life are all exquisite, unique, and unrepeatable."*
>
> Daphne Rose Kingma

When suicide impacts our lives, we all need to grieve, and, as you learned in Touchstone Two, to mourn. But our grief journeys are never exactly the same. Despite what you may hear, you will do the work of mourning in your own unique way. **Do not adopt assumptions about how long your grief should last.** Just consider taking a "one-day-at-a-time" approach. Doing so allows you to mourn at your own pace. One of my personal mantras is "No reward for speed!"

This touchstone invites you to explore some of the unique reasons your grief is what it is—the "whys" of your journey through the wilderness. The whys that follow are not all of the whys in the world, of course, just some of the more common. As you write out your responses in the companion journal, my hope is that you discover an increased understanding of the uniqueness of your grief.

WHY #1:

The Circumstances of the Suicide

Obviously, the circumstances of suicide impact the terrain of your journey. I have outlined below many specific features surrounding potential aspects of your experience. As you explore these, I encourage you to reflect on those that apply to you.

NATURE OF THE DEATH IS TRAUMATIC

A suicide death is often very traumatic. You have come to grief before you are prepared to mourn. By its very nature, your grief is naturally complicated in that the death is premature and usually unexpected. The combination of sudden shock and previously mentioned taboo and stigma result in a psychic numbing to your spirit.

POTENTIAL STIGMA AND SHAME

Sadly, there is a greater level of stigma and shame surrounding the mode of death. You are at risk for feeling the need to hide the fact that it was a suicide.

POTENTIAL "WHY?" QUESTIONS/NEED TO SEEK AN EXPLANATION

The nature of the death can lead to natural "why?" questions. You may instinctively feel the death was preventable and should not have happened. (For more discussion of "whys," see pp. 47-48). You are trying to make sense of the death.

POTENTIAL SELF-BLAME/ FELT RESPONSIBILITY

As you mourn the death of someone to suicide, you may judge your own actions, attitudes, and any sense of responsibility related to the death. (For more on blame and responsibility, see p. 111).

POTENTIAL UPENDING OF YOUR "WORLD VIEW"

You may experience disruption of your assumptive world (or what is often referred to as your "world view") particularly around feeling safe and in control. For example, your beliefs that "life is predictable" and "I can keep those I love safe from harm."

POTENTIAL INVESTIGATION BY LAW ENFORCEMENT

Often, suicide deaths initially must be investigated as if a crime may have taken place. At a time when your heart is broken, you may have felt you were under suspicion and experienced being interrogated surrounding the circumstances of the death.

POTENTIAL FOCUS ON THE ACT ITSELF

Some people around you may put more focus on the act of suicide itself than on the importance of supporting you. Sometimes the first question people ask is, "How did he do it?" This can cause further wounding of your spirit and is a form of "secondary victimization."

MULTIPLE LOSSES

You may not only be mourning the death, but loss of support from some insensitive friends and family. This creates the risk of "loss overload."

SUPPORT MAY BE LACKING:

Some people do not know what to say or do, therefore they say or do nothing. The result for you is an experience of abandonment at the very time you need unconditional love.

PRESSURE COOKER PHENOMENON

Keep in mind that if your core support group is made up of people who themselves are also grieving this suicide death, you may all experience what I call the "pressure-cooker phenomenon." Everyone may need support at the same time, and because you are all grieving, each of you also has a naturally lowered capacity to be understanding of each other. This can result in the potential of heightened tension, misunderstandings, bickering, outbursts, hurt feelings, and more. If the pressure-cooker phenomenon is making it hard for you to find support within your family and friendship systems, I would encourage you to seek outside support. Consider seeking support from friends and family who live farther away or are more emotionally distant from this death. You might also consider seeing a grief-informed counselor that can provide you the support you both need and deserve. If you're comfortable with technology, online grief forums can also be helpful.

POTENTIAL RELATIONSHIP CUT-OFFS

You may find some people who literally go away and let it be known they have no desire to talk to you or support you in any way. Again, this creates more hurt on top of your overwhelming grief.

POTENTIAL DISCOVERY OF OR WITNESSING THE SUICIDE

You may have discovered the body of the person who died or even witnessed the act of suicide. This may result in you having additional needs and may require an experienced trauma or grief counselor that is familiar with what is called "trauma processing." This is not in any way to imply that something is wrong with you, but rather that your experience was so horrific that you may need special help to support you in your grief.

ANTICIPATORY GRIEF

For some suicide loss survivors there is the experience of anticipating the potential of the death under these circumstances. If someone you care about has struggled with mental health challenges or drug abuse, you may have anticipated the potential death and your coming grief long before the day of the death. You may have also experienced the griefs of all the incremental losses along the way.

Anticipatory grief is often a dark, painful, and confusing time of limbo. If you experienced anticipatory grief before the death, that "pre-grief" is part of the terrain of your grief wilderness as well.

POTENTIAL AUTOPSY

Often, a coroner will request an autopsy as standard procedure after a sudden, unexpected death. Some people have strong emotional and spiritual reservations surrounding an autopsy being carried out. If this decision is out of your hands, it can be painful.

POTENTIAL LIFE INSURANCE PROBLEMS

Many life insurance policies contain a suicide clause. This potentially prohibits any claims for a suicide during a set period of time (often two years) from the initiation of the policy. As a result, some families have difficulty collecting on these policies, leading to an additional layer of grief.

A SURVIVOR SPEAKS

"I have experienced other deaths in my life, but never one like this. So many things came together in ways that make this so hard. There seems to be so many things around the circumstance of suicide that make this so overwhelming. It's too much for any one person to cope with."

POTENTIAL MEDIA COVERAGE

Some print and television media seem to take some perverse joy in covering suicide deaths. This can be an additional source of anguish for many survivors. The public realm may have laid claim to this death, but it is still first and foremost your personal loss.

As you can see, the list of potential circumstances surrounding suicide grief are multiple and complex. I imagine there are some additional influences you can think of that have impacted you. Whatever the circumstances, you will be well served to explore them and see how they shape the terrain of your journey.

EXPRESS YOURSELF:

Go to *The Understanding Your Suicide Grief Journal* on pp. 50-53.

WHY #2:

Your Relationship with the Person Who Died by Suicide

Your relationship with the person who died was different than that person's relationship with anyone else. For example, if your spouse died, you may have been soulmates as well as husband or wife. Or perhaps the person who died was a close friend whom you loved but also had frequent disagreements or divisive conflicts with. Or maybe you were separated by physical distance from a family member or friend who died, so you weren't as close emotionally as you would have liked, yet you find yourself grieving deeply.

A SURVIVOR SPEAKS

"I had been trying to help my son for years. I always loved him, but he wasn't easy to like. I know I will always have some sadness around what I wish we could have had in our relationship."

In general, the stronger your attachment to the person who died, the more difficult your grief journey will be. It only makes sense that the closer you felt to the person who died, the more torn apart you will feel after the death. Ambivalent, rocky relationships can also be particularly hard to integrate after a death. You may feel a strong sense of "unfinished business"—things you wanted to say but never did, conflicts you wanted to resolve but didn't.

Some suicide loss survivors have also taught me that they feel a sense of betrayal, rejection, or abandonment by the person who died. Other survivors feel no sense of disloyalty or rejection. Obviously, suicide death is experienced uniquely by each one of us and has an impact on our relationship with the person who is no longer here in physical presence.

Whatever the nature and circumstances of your relationship, you are the best person to describe them. As you work on remembering, understanding, and honoring your relationship with the person who died, you will be mourning this central truth of the loss and giving yourself momentum toward healing.

EXPRESS YOURSELF:
Go to *The Understanding Your Suicide Grief Journal* on pp. 54-57.

SOULMATE GRIEF

Soulmates are any two people who share a particularly deep affinity and connection. Spouses and life partners may be soulmates, but soulmates can also be parent and child, siblings, or close friends. Again, what matters is the strength and qualities of the bond in the relationship. The shorthand soulmates often use to describe one another is "the love of my life."

If your soulmate has died by suicide, your grief journey is likely to be especially painful and difficult—more challenging than any other grief you've experienced in your life. Your wilderness may be particularly challenging. If this is the case for you, I invite you to also look into my book *When Your Soulmate Dies: A Guide to Healing Through Heroic Mourning*. The concept of heroic mourning will offer you additional support and encouragement as you experience your grief.

WHY #3:
The People in Your Life

Mourning the death of someone to suicide requires the outside support of other human beings. Because suicide is a topic where many people don't know how to support you, some people in your world will probably pull away. This potential lack of support can be painful and agonizing.

To integrate suicide grief into your life demands an environment of empathy, caring, non-judgment, and gentle encouragement. The good news is that even one compassionate, supportive person can be a real difference-maker for you. Find a trusted family member, friend, fellow survivor, or grief-informed counselor to companion you through the terrain of your grief. This person can and will help you survive at a time you are not sure you can.

Yes, I recognize that asking for support can be more challenging than it may sound. Early in grief it is a major accomplishment to get your feet out of bed and take a shower, let alone have the capacity to reach out for help. Yet, you need and deserve unconditional love and support (see Touchstone Eight, p. 201, for more on seeking support).

Sometimes other people will assume you have a support system when you don't. For example, you may have family members and friends who live near you, but you discover they have little, if any, compassion or patience for you and your grief. Sadly, some people (in an effort to protect their own emotions) like to assume you should be "over it" and "put the past in the past." In addition, some people tend to create an environment of mutual pretense. This is where they know it was a suicide death, you know it was a suicide death, yet the unstated rule is: Don't talk about it! When this happens, a vital ingredient to your eventual healing is missing.

At the other end of the spectrum, do look for people who are more willing to patiently help you by listening without criticism or judgment. Those people know you are the expert of your own experience and gently allow you to teach them where you are in the terrain of your wilderness. They know to use the name of the person who died and realize you may need to re-tell your story over and over. They often offer, when you are ready, to locate a support group or a counselor to help you on your path. In my experience, these compassionate people have often been impacted by suicide at some point in their own lives.

Even when you're fortunate enough to have a solid support system in place, do you find that you are willing and able to accept support? If you project a need to "be strong", "carry on" and "keep your chin up," you may end up isolating yourself from the very people who would most like to walk with you in your journey through the wilderness of your grief.

EXPRESS YOURSELF:
Go to *The Understanding Your Suicide Grief Journal* on pp. 58-61.

IS YOUR GRIEF COMPLICATED?

All grief is complex and challenging, but sometimes certain losses and life experiences give rise to "complicated grief." Complicated grief is simply normal grief that has been made extra difficult by certain circumstances, such as unexpected, premature deaths including suicide; concurrent mental health challenges in the mourner; a history of abuse or addiction in the relationship; other simultaneous, major stressors in the mourner's life; and many more. Complicated grief in the aftermath of a traumatic event is also called "traumatic grief."

We'll be talking more about complicated grief in Touchstone Eight, but in the meantime, if it seems your grief and life circumstances are totally overwhelming, or if you feel stuck, in constant despair, or unable to function in your day-to-day life, you may be experiencing complicated or traumatic grief. If this is the case for you, I urge you to reach out for help right away from your primary-care provider as well as a compassionate grief counselor.

Rest assured that you're not ill, and you don't have a disorder. Rather, you're experiencing a normal response to an abnormally difficult situation—one that would likely overwhelm anyone's capacity to cope. You have severe symptoms because you've suffered a severe injury. So please—get the intensive care you need and deserve.

WHY #4:

Your Unique Personality

What words would you use to describe yourself? What words would people use to describe you? Are you a serious person? Light-hearted? Quiet and deeply reflective? Are you a nurturer? A fixer? Are you openly expressive or do you tend to naturally inhibit your emotions? In other words, what is your personality like?

Whatever your unique personality, rest assured it will be reflected in your grief. For example, if you are quiet by nature, you may express your grief quietly. If you tend to be expressive, you may openly express how you feel about your grief.

PERSONALITY TYPES

Your grief will be expressed in your natural style of relating. I have outlined several different personality types below. See if one describes you more than another.

The Thinker: This personality often tries to stay in their head, seeing the world through rational thought. They may see expressing emotions as being "soft" and not serving much purpose.

The Feeler: This personality is highly sensitive and intuitive. Other people might perceive them as "overly-emotional" or "very sensitive."

The Stoic: This personality is the strong and silent type. It may seem like there is a barrier between them and what is going on around them.

How you have responded to other changes, losses, or crises in your life may be consistent with how you respond to this death. If you tend to run away from stressful aspects of life, you may have an instinct to do the same thing now. If, however, you have always confronted crisis head on and openly, you may walk right into the center of the wilderness.

Other aspects of your personality—such as your self-esteem, values, and beliefs—also impact your response to the death. In addition, any preexisting mental health history will probably influence your grief as well.

Keep in mind there is no one right and only way to mourn. Part of your experience will be to accept that you are mourning in ways that reflect your unique personality.

EXPRESS YOURSELF:
Go to *The Understanding Your Suicide Grief Journal* on pp. 61-63.

WHY #5:

The Unique Personality of the Person Who Died by Suicide

Just as your own personality is reflected in your grief journey, so, too, is the unique personality of the person who died. What was the person who died like? What role(s) did they play in your life? Was he the funny one? Or was she the responsible one?

Really, personality is the sum total of all the characteristics that made this person who he or she was. The way she talked, the way he smiled, the way she ate her food, the way he worked, the way she related to the world around her—all these and so many more little things go into creating personality. It's no wonder there's so much to miss and that grief is so naturally complex when all these little things are gone all at once. Also, depending on the relationship you had, there may be things about the person that you don't miss.

So ask yourself: What do I miss about this person? What, if anything, do I not miss? Is there anything I wish I could have changed (but realize I couldn't) about his or her personality?

Whatever your feelings are about the personality of the person who died by suicide, find someone who will encourage you to talk about him or her openly and honestly. The key is finding someone you can trust who will listen to you without sitting in judgment of you.

Yes, authentic mourning requires you be open about what you miss and what you don't miss about this person's personality. If you don't have someone who can listen to you, at the very least write about it in the accompanying journal.

EXPRESS YOURSELF:
Go to *The Understanding Your Suicide Grief Journal* on pp. 64-69.

WHY #6:
Your Gender

Gender norms and social constructs may not only influence your grief but also the ways in which others relate to you at this time. Historically, men in Western cultures have been encouraged and expected to be "strong" and restrained, for example. As a result, they have often had more difficulty in allowing themselves to embrace and express painful feelings and accept support. Women, on the other hand, have been discouraged from expressing anger but expected to cry and show vulnerability.

A SURVIVOR SPEAKS

"He struggled with depression for years, but when he told a joke, he got this huge smile on his face. Yep, that is what I miss so very much, that big smile that could make me so happy to be around him."

Thank goodness these walls are crumbling. As our cultural understanding of gender and gender norms is evolving, grieving people are getting to be grieving people—and that is as it should be. Your feelings are your feelings, regardless of your sex or gender identification. And I believe all people are born with the instinct to grieve and mourn.

But because most of us have also, over the course of our lives, internalized deep-seated cultural stereotypes about gender and emotions, I simply ask that you try to become aware of them. This is especially true if and when they may be hindering your capacity to be present to your genuine grief and express it authentically, without shame or self-judgment.

EXPRESS YOURSELF:
Go to *The Understanding Your Suicide Grief Journal* on pp. 70-71.

WHY #7:

Your Cultural/Ethnic/Religious/Spiritual/ Philosophical Background

Your cultural and ethnic background as well as your personal belief system can have a tremendous impact on your journey into grief. When I say culture, I mean the values, rules (spoken and unspoken), and traditions that guide you and your family. Often these values, rules, and traditions have been handed down generation after generation and are shaped by the countries or areas of the world your family originally came from.

A SURVIVOR SPEAKS

"I was always told that to be a man, you shouldn't cry. But now I have no choice but to cry. If I don't, I will come apart at the seams."

For example, some cultures are more expressive of feelings (Italian, Irish), whereas others may be more stoic (English, German). Again, while we want to avoid the trap of over-generalizing, ask yourself how the culture that has been passed down to you influences your grief.

Your religious or spiritual or philosophical life might be deepened, challenged, renewed, or changed as part of your grief experience. Suicide grief can naturally disrupt the spiritual terrain of your life, and you may well find yourself questioning your beliefs as part of your work of mourning.

As you are probably aware, suicide has a long and complex history with religion. It wasn't all that long ago that suicide was thought to be a sin by almost all major faiths. Fortunately, in contemporary times and surrounded by much information and education, suicide is no longer considered a sin by the majority of world religions. Many, but not all, communities of faith offer compassion and support to survivors. If you are part of a faith community, I certainly hope that is your experience. If not, be assured that there are many faith communities that can and will support you in your grief.

Let me be very direct with you—if you turn to a clergyperson for support and he or she tells you that suicide is an unpardonable sin, go someplace else to get the support and non-judgment you both need and deserve. And remember what someone wise once said, "The God I have come to believe in is not in the judging business." Find someone to support you who is a good fit for your spiritual needs right now. Also, if you are not a person of religion, don't allow people to force you to "find God" or seek out religious answers that do not speak to you. Your journey through the terrain of your healing is yours alone, and the paths you take to do that are up to you.

Yes, when someone you are connected to dies by suicide, you may feel very close to God or a Higher Power, or you may feel distant, perhaps even hostile. You may find yourself asking questions such as, "Why has this happened to me?" or "Where is God in this?" When you are faced with a suicide, you are faced with mystery. No, you may not discover answers to your questions about faith or spirituality, but that doesn't mean you should not ask them. After all, the greatest religious figures in history have done this very same thing. As I mentioned earlier in this book, mystery is actually the ancient name for God. God can handle your questions.

Faith means to believe in something for which there is no proof. For some people, faith means believing in and following a set of religious rules. For others, faith is a belief in God, a spiritual presence, or a force that is greater than we are. Whatever your beliefs, in befriending the mystery surrounding the suicide of someone in your life, there is an acknowledgment that certain things cannot be changed. Yet, even as the reality of the death cannot be altered, you and I can have hope for our healing.

I would be remiss if I didn't warn you to be alert to people who project that if you "have faith," you can bypass the need to mourn. If you internalize this misconception (see page 54), you will set yourself up to grieve internally but not mourn externally. **Having faith does not mean you do not need to mourn. Having faith does mean having the courage to allow yourself to mourn!**

With the death of someone to suicide comes a natural "search for meaning" (see page 144 for more exploration about this). You have probably found yourself re-evaluating your life based on this loss. You will benefit from finding someone who is willing and able to honor your need to explore your religious/spiritual/philosophical values, question your attitude toward life, and support you unconditionally as you renew your resources for living. This part of the terrain of your grief takes time, and it may well lead to some changes in your values, beliefs, and lifestyle.

EXPRESS YOURSELF:
Go to *The Understanding Your Suicide Grief Journal* on pp. 71-74.

WHY #8:

Other Changes, Challenges, or Stresses in Your Life Right Now

What else is going on in your life right now? Although we often think it shouldn't, the earth does keep turning

A SURVIVOR SPEAKS

"I have to change some of what I call my 'faith friends.' Some people have had the nerve to tell me my wife is now in hell. That is not my God. So I have had to be careful whom I spend time with. My best friends are now what I call my 'nonjudgmental friends.'"

after the death of someone loved. You may still have to work and manage finances. Other people in your life may be sick or in need of help of some kind. You may have children or elderly parents to care for (or both!). You may have too many commitments and too little time and energy to complete them.

Whatever your specific situation, I'm sure that your grief is not the only stress in your life right now. And the more intense and numerous the other current stresses in your life, the more overwhelming your grief journey may be.

If at all possible, take steps to de-stress your life for the time being. Give up optional obligations and defer any unnecessary projects. Now is the time to concentrate on mourning and being self-compassionate.

EXPRESS YOURSELF:
Go to *The Understanding Your Suicide Grief Journal* on pp. 74-76.

WHY #9:

Your Experiences with Loss and Death in the Past

One way to think about yourself is that you are the sum total of all that you have experienced in your life so far. One "why?" of your response to this death is your past loss history. Perhaps this is your very first experience with death, particularly a sudden, traumatic death. In contrast, some people experience a series of deaths and are overwhelmed by these multiple losses. What about you? Also, what other non-death related losses have you experienced in the past?

Regardless of your prior loss experiences, there is little that can

A SURVIVOR SPEAKS

"I have had three deaths in the last sixteen months, this last one being a suicide. I have had to get help because I'm not just mourning one death. I have discovered each death is so unique."

prepare you for the wilderness you are now in. However, I have found that it is helpful to invite you to reflect on your history of losses and consider how they influence, if at all, your current journey into grief.

EXPRESS YOURSELF:
Go to *The Understanding Your Suicide Grief Journal* on pp. 76-77.

TOO MUCH LOSS

Unfortunately, some people (maybe you) experience more than one loss in a short period of time. A suicide death may result in a ripple effect of loss (see misconception, p. 55). Or, a suicide may be experienced in close proximity to another death in your life. In addition, other types of losses— job changes, divorce, illness, children leaving home—can sometimes take place on top of the suicide death.

The grief of loss overload is different from typical grief because it is emanating from more than one loss and because it is jumbled. Our minds and hearts have enough trouble coping with one loss at a time, but when they have to deal with multiple losses simultaneously, the grief often seems especially chaotic and defeating. Before you can mourn one loss, here comes another loss. Even if you have coped with grief effectively in the past, you may be finding that this time it's different. This time you may feel like you're struggling to survive.

If you have suffered multiple losses and are struggling with grief overload, I encourage you to work with a grief-informed counselor. Even if you have empathetic friends and listeners in your life, you need and deserve extra support. An experienced, compassionate grief counselor can help you create a plan for sorting and mourning the separate losses. Each will need its own time and attention, and a counselor can help you navigate the process in ways you will find helpful.

To learn more about grief overload, see my book *Too Much Loss: Coping with Grief Overload*.

WHY #10:

Your Physical and Mental Health

How you feel physically and mentally has a significant effect on your grief. If you are tired and eating poorly, your coping skills will be diminished. If you were dealing with physical or mental health issues before the death, your symptoms may now be exacerbated.

We'll discuss this important issue further in Touchstone Seven. For now, bear in mind that taking care of yourself physically and mentally is one of the best things you can do to lay the foundation for healthy, authentic mourning.

A SURVIVOR SPEAKS

"The month after my father's suicide death, my young son was diagnosed with a chronic asthma condition, and then three weeks after that my favorite uncle died from a heart attack. Fortunately, I knew I couldn't survive this alone and sought out the help of a counselor and a support group."

EXPRESS YOURSELF:
Go to *The Understanding Your Suicide Grief Journal* on p. 78.

WHY #11:

The Ceremony or Funeral Experience

Because suicide death is sudden and usually unexpected, it becomes even more important to participate in meaningful ceremonies or funerals. I often say, "When words are inadequate, have a ceremony." Unfortunately, because of the taboo and stigma that can surround death by suicide, some people may have discouraged you from having a funeral at the time of the death. The good news is that it is never too late to use ceremony as part of your self-care.

There is no single, right way to have a funeral. We do know, however, that holding a meaningful ceremony can aid you in your social, emotional, and spiritual healing after a death. Keep in mind that funerals are not really rites of closure, but rather rites of initiation.

Funerals are a time and a place to express your feelings about the death. The funeral also can serve as a time to honor the person who died, bring you closer to others who can give you needed support, affirm that life goes on even in the face of death, and give you a context of meaning that is in keeping with your own religious, spiritual, or philosophical background. **In short, a meaningful funeral experience can help put you on a path to eventually integrating the loss into your life.**

If you were unable to attend the funeral of the person who died, or if the funeral was minimized, distorted, or nonexistent, you may find that this complicates your grief experience. Be assured, however, that it is never too late after a death to plan and carry out a ceremony (even a second or third ceremony can be helpful with suicide grief) that will help meet your needs. For example, you might choose to have a tree-planting ceremony in the spring in honor of the person who died. Or you might elect to hold a memorial service on the anniversary of the death. The power of ceremony is that it helps people heal. You deserve ceremony, and so do the other people mourning this death. For more on the power of ceremony to facilitate mourning, see page 146.

EXPRESS YOURSELF:
Go to *The Understanding Your Suicide Grief Journal* on pp. 79-80.

What else has shaped your unique grief journey? There are probably other factors, large and small, that are influencing your grief right now. What are they? I invite you to think about them and to write about them in your companion journal.

THE IMPORTANCE OF TELLING YOUR STORY

A vital part of healing in grief is often "telling the story" over and over again.

The story of the life of the person who died, the times you shared, and their death comprises many or all of the "whys" we've been reviewing in this touchstone. I find that the two major backward-looking "whys" that grievers naturally give attention to are their relationship with the person who died and the circumstances of the death. But your story may include bits of all the "whys" and other things as well.

It's normal and necessary to tell this story. The more you tell it, the more it starts to come together into a coherent narrative with a beginning, middle, and end. The more you tell it, the deeper your acknowledgment of the loss becomes and the more you begin to discover some level of understanding and reconciliation with what happened.

What if you don't want to talk about it? It's OK to respect this self-protective instinct for a while, but at some point, you will probably be well served to start talking about it. Keeping your thoughts and feelings about the death inside you only makes them more powerful. Over time, your grief story will likely evolve from one dominated by the death to one dominated by memories of the person who died. This is a natural progression and a sign that you are integrating the loss into your life.

Find people who are willing to listen to you tell your story, over and over again if necessary, without judgment. But remember that not everyone has the capacity to be an empathetic listener. Seek out listeners who can be present to your pain and who don't mind if you need to repeat yourself often in the days, weeks, and months ahead.

Moving from Whys to Whats

My hope is that Touchstone Three has helped you understand why your grief is being experienced the way it is. But what is even more fundamental for you to be attuned to is what your thoughts and feelings are. What are you feeling today? What have you been thinking about for the last day or two?

A big part of healing in grief is learning to listen and attend to your inner voice and to give those thoughts and feelings expression as you experience them. In the next touchstone we will discuss some of these common and varied thoughts and feelings.

Explore Your Feelings of Loss

> *"Emotions are a language. Every emotion means something. When you understand the language, you suddenly gain incredible insight into yourself and others."*
>
> Scot Conway

On your journey through the wilderness of your grief, a critical trail marker to be on the watch for is Touchstone Four, which guides you in exploring your many and varied feelings of loss. Actually, this fourth touchstone colors all the others, because your emotions shape what each of the other touchstones feel like for you.

Stepping into the wilderness of your many feelings of grief is an important and sacred part of your life right now. It is my experience that we cannot heal what we cannot feel or do not allow ourselves to feel. Being in the wilderness of your emotions invites you to get to know your authentic self and feel the depth of your response to the suicide death of someone in your life.

Suicide grief creates profound disruption in almost all areas of your life. It challenges all you know about yourself and the world around you. This journey rocks the complete foundation of your entire being. Suicide is synonymous with disruption, chaos, and change—all of which bring a multitude of overwhelming emotions. **Taking ownership of your wilderness emotions is the only way to eventually re-orient and survive this life-changing experience.** As your companion, I urge you to remember: Out of the darkness will eventually come light! Be patient, be steadfast, and be self-compassionate as we explore this important touchstone.

The Importance of Experiencing and Expressing Your Feelings

As overwhelming as your emotions may seem, they are true expressions of where you are in the terrain of your journey. **Rather than deny, inhibit, self-treat, or go around them (all of which**

can be tempting to want to do), I want to help you recognize and learn from them. Yes, as I noted in Touchstone One, it's actually this process of becoming friendly with your feelings that will help you heal – or become whole again – all the time knowing you have been changed forever by this experience. In some ways I have found it helpful to think of our feelings as our teachers. The healing of the wounds of suicide grief starts with an awareness of our feelings. So, as much as you may want to run from your feelings of profound grief, I gently encourage you to be open to your teachers!

Now, some people say to me, "What is the point of experiencing and expressing feelings if they don't change anything?" I get this question often from people experiencing the grief that accompanies suicide.

It's true that experiencing your feelings and talking about your feelings does not change what you are going through. However, self-expression does have the capacity to change you and the way you see the world around you. Putting your feelings into words gives them meaning and shape. Feelings are certainly not punishments, they are information. Remember, you have been "torn apart" and have some very unique needs. Allow me the privilege of helping you reconstruct yourself.

Authentic mourning creates what is called perturbation, which is "the capacity to experience change and movement." The word *feeling* originates from the Indo-European root word and literally means "touch." So, it is in expressing your feelings that you activate your capacity to be touched and changed by experiences you encounter along life's path.

As a result, to be able to integrate the grief that comes with suicide requires that you are touched by what you experience. When you cannot, or choose not to, feel your feelings, you become closed in your ability to use or be changed by them. Instead of experiencing movement, you become stuck.

Actually, feelings have one ambition in life—to be felt. Emotions want and try to demand motion. However, if you deny, inhibit, or self-treat your feelings, your pain will last longer. Honoring feelings is the same as being honest and accepting feelings. **I always remind people I companion in grief that feelings wait on welcome, not on time.**

To express means, in part, to press out, to make known, to reveal. When we have strong feelings and we don't express them, we risk exploding. I don't want you to explode. Expression actually allows you a kind of freedom: the freedom to recognize and integrate your emotions in their fullest form.

Please don't think of your feelings as "negative;" instead, think of them as necessary. If you perceive some of your feelings, such as anger, sadness, and anxiety, as negative, you will not gain anything helpful from them. To ultimately integrate this loss into your life, you will be required to drop any conditioning or judgments that your emotions are negative. Being open to the healing you will eventually experience means, in part, being open to any and all of your feelings.

This expression of feelings that brings release from the risk of explosion even has another fancy-sounding term: *catharsis.* Catharsis is a Greek word meaning "purging" or "purification." It is the process of bringing feelings to consciousness.

The beauty of this process is that you don't even need to understand what you are feeling in order to express it. You will have time down the line to sort out the texture of your many feelings and explore their origins. For now, let's just create an opportunity for you to befriend whatever thoughts and feelings you are having.

My hope is that this touchstone will help you see how natural your many thoughts, feelings, and behaviors are. I have companioned thousands of suicide survivors, and they have taught me about this journey. I have also walked this walk myself. One of the most important things I have learned is that the eventual healing that we experience as survivors is not a task, it is a need. It simply requires your engagement.

Rest assured that whatever your thoughts and feelings, while in one sense they are completely unique to you, they are also usually a common human response to a suicide death. Questions throughout this section of your companion journal will encourage you to see how a particular feeling I am describing is, has been, or will be, a part of your personal experience. Your journal is one place to describe your experience and familiarize yourself with various dimensions of your unique journey—to tell your story.

A SURVIVOR SPEAKS

"As hard as it is to do, I have learned I have to feel my grief to heal my grief. Part of me wanted to deny my feelings of loss and try to put this behind me. It simply didn't work. The grief was so powerful and overwhelming that it demanded my attention."

As you explore the feelings that relate to your journey, remember that what you are doing is a vital part of your eventual healing. Keep in mind that although you may not have experienced some of the thoughts and feelings described in this touchstone, you may in the future. In addition, a reminder that these dimensions of potential feelings may be part of your experience, but they don't unfold neatly in an orderly and predictable way.

Shock, Psychic Numbing, Dissociation, Denial, Disbelief

When you first learn of a suicide death, it is instinctive to need to push away your new reality. By the time you have picked up this book and are reading, your initial shock has likely softened.

However, as you look back on some of your initial responses, you will probably be able to relate to many of the following aspects of your experience.

"It feels like a bad dream," people in early grief from a suicide death often say. "I feel like I might wake up and this will not have happened." Looking back, there is often a total sense of unreality.

Thank goodness for shock, numbness, and disbelief! Other words that survivors use to describe their initial grief are dazed and stunned. These feelings are nature's way of temporarily protecting you from the full reality of the sudden, unexpected death. They help insulate you psychologically until you are more able to tolerate what you don't want to believe. In essence, these feelings serve as a "temporary time-out" or a "psychological shock absorber."

Trauma loss from suicide often goes beyond what might be considered "normal" shock. In fact, you may experience what is called "psychic numbing"—the deadening or shutting off of emotions. Your sense that "this isn't happening to me" often continues much longer than with other circumstances of death.

Psychic numbing is like a bandage that your psyche has placed over your wound. The bandage protects the wound until it becomes less open and raw. Only after some necessary time and a scab forms is the bandage removed and the wound openly exposed to the world.

Especially in the beginning of your grief journey, your emotions need time to catch up with what your mind has been told. Even when it is clear that the death was from suicide, you may find yourself needing to deny this fact. In a very real sense, it is a way of holding off the pain and suffering that is coming soon enough.

On one level, you may realize the facts don't lie about the suicide and know the person is dead. But on other, deeper levels, you are not able and willing to truly believe it. This mixture of shock, psychic numbing, dissociation, and disbelief acts as an anesthetic. The pain exists, but fortunately you may not experience it fully.

Some suicide loss survivors experience what is called dissociation – a feeling of separation or distance from what is happening around you. This is when you feel like you are there but not there. Or, that you are somehow disconnected from experiences that you're right in the middle of. Dissociation can be an aspect of shock. It may feel strange and even scary sometimes, but it's common and normal.

In early grief, you may also feel a sense of surrealness. Surreal means bizarre, irrational, even make-believe. Your mind interprets that what is happening can't actually be happening because it is not possible for it to be real. "It feels like a dream," grievers often say. "I feel like I might wake up and none of this will have happened." That dreamlike aspect of early grief is surrealness. It often feels overwhelming and can be naturally disconcerting, but it happens to many people after a death to suicide.

You may have found yourself crying uncontrollably, having angry outbursts, repeating the word "why?", or even fainting. These are all normal and necessary responses that can help you survive this sudden, unexpected death. Typically, a physiological component accompanies feelings of shock. Your autonomic nervous system takes over and may cause heart palpitations, queasiness, stomach pain, tightness in the throat, shortness of breath, and dizziness.

Unfortunately, some people may try to squelch these normal responses, believing you should be "in control." They may try to quiet you in an effort to feel more comfortable themselves. Yet, this is a naturally out-of-control, uncomfortable time for you. You have had to come to grief before you were prepared to mourn. Trying to "control" yourself would mean suppressing your intuitive response to this sudden death. Don't do it. Remember—your needs are the priority right now, not theirs. During this vulnerable time you will do what you need to do to survive.

As you look back on this time of your journey, you may not remember specific words that were spoken to you. Your mind was blocking; it heard but could not listen. Although you may not remember some, or any, of the words other people are telling you, you may remember who you felt comforted by and who you didn't feel support from. This is a time when non-verbal, compassionate presence is more important than any words that could be spoken.

Denial is often one of the most misunderstood aspects of the grief experience after a suicide death. Temporarily, elements of denial, like shock, psychic numbing and dissociation, are a great gift. They help you survive. However, denial should soften over time as you mourn and as you acknowledge, slowly and in doses, that the person is really dead. While denial is helpful—even necessary—early in your grief, ongoing denial clearly blocks the path to healing. For more exploration of this critical topic, see p. 34 under Touchstone One where I outline the important distinctions between shock and denial. At bottom, if you cannot accept the reality of the death, you cannot mourn it in ways that allow for healing.

Often in suicide grief, denial goes on at one level of awareness while acknowledgment of the reality of the death goes on at another level. Your mind may approach and retreat from the reality of the death over and over again as you try to integrate the death into your life. This back-and-forth process is normal and necessary. I describe it as "Evade – Encounter." The key is to not get stuck permanently on evade. Active mourning is a slow but necessary process of adjusting to a painful loss, and until the pain can be experienced in doses, mourning cannot unfold.

Remember—even after you have moved beyond the initial shock, psychic numbing, dissociation, denial, and disbelief, don't be surprised if this constellation of experiences resurfaces sometimes. Birthdays, anniversaries, holidays, and other special occasions that may only be known to you often create a resurgence of shock. You may suddenly realize that this person who was so much a part of your life is no longer there to share these days with. When this happens, a flood of shock and numbness may be experienced in a wave-like fashion.

SELF-CARE SUGGESTIONS

At this point you probably realize that shock, psychic numbing, dissociation, denial, and disbelief are not things you can prevent yourself from experiencing. Instead, you can be grateful that these shock absorbers have been available to you at a time when you have needed them most. So, be compassionate with yourself. Allow for these instinctive forms of self-protection. This dimension of grief provides a much needed, but temporary, means of dosing yourself as a new reality sets in.

A primary self-care principle during this time is to reach out for support from caring friends, family, fellow survivors, and caregivers you trust. When you are in shock, your instinctive response is to have other people care for you. Let them. Try to allow yourself to be nurtured even if your instinct is to push people away.

A SURVIVOR SPEAKS

"I felt like a robot—detached and alone. I just kept saying 'This cannot be happening, no way!' It was like I was watching myself from the outside in. Now, I realize my feelings of shock and numbness helped me survive my early grief."

However, accepting support does not mean being totally passive and doing nothing for yourself. Actually, having someone take over completely is usually not helpful. Given appropriate support and understanding, you will find value in doing some things for yourself. In other words, don't allow anyone to do for you what you want to do for yourself.

You may find that some people feel a need to bring you too quickly to the complete reality of what you are faced with. They may say things like, "You just have to admit it and then go on... put it in the past...other people need you." I have noted as a theme that your ultimate healing does require acknowledging the reality of the death from suicide. However, this is probably not the time to embrace the full depth of your loss or move forward quickly and efficiently. Fortunately, the function of shock usually won't allow you to move too quickly even if you thought it wise to do so. If others insist on taking away your early need to push away some of the full reality of what confronts you, ignore or set boundaries with them. As challenging as it is, over time and with self-compassion, allow the reality of this suicide death to gently make movement from head awareness to heart awareness.

EXPRESS YOURSELF:
Go to *The Understanding Your Suicide Grief Journal* on pp. 85-87.

SAYING ALOUD THE WORD *SUICIDE*

One very helpful way to begin to move from head to heart related to shock is to start incorporating the word suicide into the language that you use. I realize that acknowledging you are a suicide loss survivor may take some time, so do be gentle with yourself. However, making actual statements such as "_____ died by suicide," helps you acknowledge the reality. You then set the tone for others to talk about it and prevent the tendency to create mutual pretense, which is where you know it was suicide and people around you know it was suicide, but nobody acknowledges that reality.

Using the person's name honors that he or she lived and prevents the all-too-common phenomenon of the "family secret." Remember: suicide is death by just another name. Do not internalize the stigma often inspired by a society that often doesn't understand or know how to support you. Yes, use the person's name, and use the word suicide. Doing so is a reflection that love doesn't end with death and that you are helping yourself and people around you by acknowledging your reality.

Disorganization, Confusion, Searching, Yearning

Perhaps the most isolating and frightening part of your grief journey is the sense of disorganization, confusion, searching, and yearning that often comes with the death of someone to suicide. These experiences often arise when you begin to confront the reality of the death. As one survivor expressed to me, "I cannot stay focused on anything. My mind jumps from one thought to the next, and I'm lucky to just remember my name."

This dimension of grief may give rise to what I call the "going crazy syndrome." I have had many suicide survivors say, "I think I'm going crazy." That's because in grief, thoughts and behaviors are different from what you normally experience. If you feel disorganized and confused, know that you are not going crazy, you are in the midst of grief and need to mourn. To further your understanding of the "going crazy syndrome," see Touchstone Six.

You may feel a sense of restlessness, agitation, impatience, and ongoing confusion. It's like being in the middle of a wild, rushing river where you can't get a grasp on anything. Or, to use a wilderness metaphor, you are in the middle of a dark forest, and no matter which way you turn, you cannot seem to find your way out.

You may express disorganization and confusion in your inability to complete tasks. You may start to do something but have trouble finishing it. You may feel forgetful and think you have totally lost your memory.

Disconnected thoughts may race through your mind, and a multitude of strong emotions may be overwhelming. This is usually accompanied by what is called *anhedonia*—the inability to find joy in things that previously brought you joy. Historically, this was referred to as "melancholia" and we understood this as a normal response to loss.

You may also experience a restless searching for the person who died by suicide. After someone dies, it is normal to look for them and expect them to reappear. Yearning and preoccupation with memories can leave you feeling drained. If you discovered the body or witnessed the suicide death, this part of your grief can be naturally complicated.

If your mind is impacted by recurring and unwanted images, please seek help immediately from someone trained to assist you. (See information on Post-Traumatic Stress Disorder on the next page).

During this time you may experience a shift in perception: other people may begin to look like the person in your life who died by suicide. You might be at a store, look down an aisle, and think you see the person. Or you might see a familiar car drive past you and find yourself wanting to follow the car. Some survivors report things such as thinking they heard the garage door open and the person entering the house as he or she had done so many times before. If experiences similar to these are happening or have happened to you, remember—you are not crazy!

Visual hallucinations occur so frequently that they can't be considered abnormal. I personally prefer the term "memory picture" to hallucination. As part of your searching and yearning when you're in grief, you may not only experience a sense of the dead person's presence, but you also may have fleeting glimpses of the person across a room.

You may also dream about the person who died. Dreams can be an unconscious means of searching for this person. Be careful not to over-interpret your dreams. Simply remain open to learning from them. If the dreams are pleasant, embrace them; if they are disturbing or you feel haunted by them, find someone who can support and help you. If you are consistently having nightmares and feel tormented, please see a grief-informed counselor as soon as possible.

UNDERSTANDING POST-TRAUMATIC STRESS DISORDER

Post-traumatic stress disorder, or PTSD, is a term used to describe the psychological condition that survivors of sudden, violent death sometimes experience. People with PTSD may have nightmares or scary thoughts about the traumatic experience they or the person who died by suicide went through.

If you're experiencing PTSD, you may suffer from chronic feelings of shock or helplessness. You may avoid most people and situations that remind you of the death, sometimes even becoming housebound. You might feel angry, nervous, afraid, and tense. You might be on the lookout for danger and get very upset when something happens without warning. You may startle easily, for example, when someone comes to the door or a phone rings. Your anxiety level may be continually high.

Suicide grief and PTSD can overlap in some ways with each other. I often refer to suicide grief as naturally complicated grief, and you can probably see how easily PTSD and your journey into grief can interface. If you think you may be suffering from PTSD, talk to your primary care provider or a trauma counselor who can help you get the help you need and deserve. Some people need help with their PTSD before their authentic mourning can unfold.

It may be helpful for you to know that your response to trauma and to the potential onset of PTSD symptoms has more to do with the intensity and duration of the stressful events in your life than with your personality. Don't think you are "weak" if this suicide experience and its repercussions have overwhelmed your coping resources. Don't feel ashamed if you need professional help.

Do keep in mind that many suicide loss survivors are traumatized without meeting the formal criteria for PTSD. You may have anxiety and anger. You may flow in and out of shock and experience feelings of helplessness. You may feel a need to withdraw at times to restore yourself. You may think

(continued on next page)

about the experience of the death a lot. You are probably in great pain. But if you are still able to function in your daily life and interact lovingly with others, you may not have what gets referred to as PTSD. Still, you may well be naturally traumatized by the suicide and in need of, and deserving of, special care and consideration, both from yourself and from others.

WARNING: Some traditionally trained mental health counselors who may not have specialized training in trauma grief may be quick to diagnose you with PTSD. So, I simply urge you to check out the qualifications of the person you seek help from and get assurance they have specialized training in trauma grief. I note this because the word "disorder" is frightening to many survivors. By its very nature, suicide grief is complicated and often mimics many of the symptoms of PTSD. It is a real phenomenon, but I don't want you to think you are some kind of "disordered" person. You are a normal person having a normal response to an abnormal, infrequent, traumatic experience in your life. For further understanding, see my book *The PTSD Solution* wherein I reframe PTSD as traumatic grief.

Other common experiences during this time include difficulties with eating and sleeping. You may experience a loss of appetite, or you may find yourself overeating. Even when you do eat, you may be unable to taste the food. Having trouble falling asleep, disruption of your sleep during the night, and early morning awakening are also common during this dimension of your grief experience.

Many suicide survivors express concern to me that they are not sleeping and eating normally. Actually, I would be shocked if as a suicide loss survivor you were sleeping and eating as you did prior to this death. Just as other dimensions of your grief will soften over time, you can look forward to a return to your prior sleeping and eating behaviors. Right now you will be well served to be self-compassionate and patient with yourself.

Another way to understand this dimension is through a discussion of the five areas in which stress impacts your life: physical, cognitive, emotional, social and spiritual. The stress of being a suicide loss survivor affects each of these areas of your life:

- Physically: your body feels exhausted.
- Cognitively: your mind has trouble concentrating and staying focused.
- Emotionally: your feelings are intense and overwhelming.
- Socially: your relationships require energy that you often don't have.
- Spiritually: you may question the meaning and purpose of your life.

If you are feeling stressed in all five areas (and most survivors do), it is no wonder you encounter aspects of disorganization and confusion! Fortunately, these five areas and what you can do to help yourself with them are explored in Touchstone Seven.

A SURVIVOR SPEAKS

"As I look back, I realize I was so confused I didn't know which way was up. At first I was impatient with myself, but then I learned to slow down and be more gentle with myself. That made all the difference."

Also, keep in mind that whenever we as human beings experience major life transitions, we encounter disorganization, confusion, and chaos on the pathway to any kind of reorganization. I often say, "All change starts with chaos." While it may seem strange, it has helped many people I have companioned in their suicide journey to remind themselves that disorganization and confusion are actually steppingstones on the path toward eventual reorganization, healing, and integration.

SELF-CARE SUGGESTIONS

If disorganization, confusion, searching, and yearning are, or have been, part of your grief journey, please realize you are not alone. As a matter of fact, as previously noted, I'd be shocked if you didn't have some of these experiences. So, remember— you have unique needs and are mourning a major life change.

The thoughts, feelings, and behaviors of this dimension do not come all at once. They are often experienced in a wave-like fashion. You might have a day or even several days where you feel more focused again and then your disorganization and confusion return suddenly and without notice. This is natural, so I urge you to not get discouraged.

During these times, you may well need to talk and cry for long periods of time. At other times you may just need to go to exile and spend some time alone.

Try not to interpret what you are thinking and feeling. Just think and feel it. **Allowing yourself to let in whatever you are experiencing is actually one of the best ways to remain in an active healing process.** Don't get defensive with yourself and shut down. If you want these natural symptoms that reflect your unique needs to soften over time, the only cushion for them to fall on is your awareness and expression. Give your disorientation the attention it deserves and demands.

When you feel disoriented, talk to someone who will be supportive and understanding. Sometimes when you talk, you may not think you make much sense. And you may not. But talking it out can still be self-clarifying, even at a subconscious level.

As difficult as it may seem to do, create a lifeline to people who are willing to listen to you tell your story, over and over again if necessary, without judgment. Better yet, make use of this book with a group of fellow mourners who have also experienced the death of someone to suicide.

If you do not participate in a support group experience, I do urge you to locate and make use of at least one person whom you feel understands and will not judge you. That person must be patient and attentive because you may revisit aspects of your experience over and over as you befriend your grief. He or she must be genuinely interested in understanding and supporting you. If someone is not able to give honor and respect to your story, find someone else who will be able to better meet your needs.

During this time, discourage yourself from making any critical decisions, such as selling the house, quitting your job, or moving to another place. Because of the judgment-making difficulties that naturally come with this part of the journey, ill-timed, premature decisions might result in more loss on top of loss. Go slow and be patient with yourself. Sometimes suicide loss survivors unconsciously try to push away pain and confusion by moving to action too quickly. Remember one of my favorite mantras: "No rewards for speed!"

EXPRESS YOURSELF:
Go to *The Understanding Your Suicide Grief Journal* on pp. 88-90.

Anxiety, Panic, Fear

Feelings of anxiety, panic, and fear may be part of your grief experience. You may ask yourself, "Am I going to be okay? Will I survive this? Will I be so overwhelmed that I, too, would take my own life? What about other family members? Might they take their own lives? Will my life have any meaning and purpose without this person?" These questions are normal. Your sense of safety and security has been threatened, and you are naturally anxious.

THOUGHTS ON RESILIENCE

Resilience is often defined as the capacity to bounce back after difficult life losses and transitions. When you're grieving, it's a concept to be aware of and watch out for.

In our mourning-avoidant culture, people sometimes put resilience on a pedestal. They may mistakenly equate it with being strong in grief and "getting over it" quickly. But that's not resilience—that's denial.

True resilience in grief doesn't mean being phony or avoiding your grief. Instead, it means intentionally choosing actions known to support healing. It means embracing the realities of grief. It means befriending and expressing all the feelings we're reviewing in this chapter. It means authentically sharing them with others. It means cultivating connection and hope.

Resilience is a skill that can be practiced and learned. Whenever you choose to think and act with authenticity, compassion, hope, and gratitude—toward yourself and others—you are cultivating true resilience.

Most important, allow me to address the issue of any fear around your own suicide or that of your family members. You now know the pain and devastation that suicide brings into the lives of survivors. The fact that you are taking time to read this book demonstrates your desire to integrate this loss into your life and go on living. This can outweigh any thoughts you have about ending your own life. If ANY thoughts persist around fear of taking your own life, I implore you to go see a professional caregiver who can assist you RIGHT NOW!

As your head and heart miss the person who was part of your life, anxiety, fear, even panic may set in. The onset of these feelings sometimes makes people think they are going crazy. Again, let me assure you that you are not going crazy; instead you are a suicide loss survivor who has been torn apart and has important needs. If you do believe you are "abnormal," your level of anxiety may continue to increase. **That is why it is so important to remind yourself that you are having a normal response to an abnormal life experience.**

Yes, right now you may feel a sense of vulnerability unlike anything you might have experienced before. You may be frightened by your inability to concentrate. You may be afraid of what your future holds or that other people in your life will go away and leave you. You may be more aware of your own mortality, which can be scary. Perhaps you are not only mourning the death, but also confronting the challenges of now trying to single parent children who also have unique needs related to the death. For some suicide loss survivors, financial problems can also compound feelings of anxiety.

Your sleep may be affected by fear at this time. Overwhelming, painful thoughts and feelings that can come in dreams or nightmares can naturally cause difficulties with sleeping.

Anxiety, fear, and panic can also be a part of your experience if you discovered the body of the person who died. This can be a traumatic and overwhelming experience that impacts your mind, body, and spirit. If you have unwanted and recurring images related to the discovery of the body, I urge you to get support from a trained professional who can help you.

Anxiety sometimes shows up in the form of panic attacks. Panic is a sudden, overpowering feeling of terror, often accompanied by physical symptoms such as a racing heart, sweating, chest pain, nausea, and more. People sometimes feel like they're dying when they experience a panic attack. Panic attacks usually only last for a few minutes, but they are often terrifying. I have seen numerous grieving people in counseling whose panic attacks were the doorway to get them to give attention to their grief and learn to authentically mourn.

While unpleasant, anxiety, fear, and yes, even panic, can be natural components of the grief experience. You may worry about small things that never concerned you before. You may fear you will never have control over your life again. Remember—you are responding normally to an experience you likely never thought you would have to face. **The good news is that expressing your fears can help make them more tolerable.** Also, recognizing that they are temporary and will soften over time can and will help you during this vulnerable time in your life.

A SURVIVOR SPEAKS

"After my son took his own life, I was immobilized by fear. I kept thinking, 'Who else might do this? My other children, my husband, even me?' Thankfully, as I got support and openly mourned, those fears went away over time."

SELF-CARE SUGGESTIONS

If anxiety, panic, and fear are a part of your grief journey, you will need to talk about them with someone who will be understanding and supportive. Conversely, not talking about these feelings makes them so much more powerful and destructive.

You will find it helpful to talk about your fears and anxieties. If you don't talk about them, you may find yourself retreating from other people and from the world in general. I have seen many grieving people become prisoners in their own homes. They repress their anxiety, panic, and fear, only to discover that these feelings are now repressing them. I encourage you to not allow your fears and anxieties to go unexpressed.

And if you are experiencing panic attacks, be sure to seek help from your primary-care provider or a grief counselor. They are simply a sign that you need some extra support.

EXPRESS YOURSELF:
Go to *The Understanding Your Suicide Grief Journal* on pp. 90-91.

Explosive Emotions

The sense of overwhelming loss that suicide brings about naturally provides fuel for the potential of what I call explosive emotions. As you come to acknowledge the reality of this death, emotions of protest often call out for expression. Many people oversimplify these protest emotions by talking only about anger. However, blame, terror, rage, and even jealousy are explosive emotions that may be part of your experience. Again—these are natural emotions, but some survivors have taught me they find them frightening, particularly when they are focused on the person who has died by suicide.

I have found that it helps to understand that all of these explosive feelings are, fundamentally, a form of protest. We know that it is actually psycho-biologically instinctive in the face of traumatic loss to protest—to dislike your new reality and want to change it in some way. Protest is an instinctive attempt to get back what you lost that you value.

You may direct your instinctive need to protest toward the person who died by suicide. "How could you abandon me, your family, your friends, and give up on living!" You may be mad at God. You may be mad at friends, family members, investigative officers, or anyone who is available. You may feel a deep visceral anger inside of you. You may feel raw and exposed. You may even be frightened by the depth of your explosive emotions.

Explosive emotions can help you survive when the world around you doesn't feel safe. It makes good sense that the emotional defense against fear is anger. This entire experience doesn't feel fair or right. It feels unfair and all wrong! Anger and these other explosive emotions can help you feel like you have some element of control at a time when you naturally feel out of control. They also help counter more passive, painful feelings of helplessness, fear, despair, and sadness.

Unfortunately, some people around you may not understand how natural and necessary your explosive emotions can be. No, you don't want to get stuck in them or have them lead to outward or inward destruction, but you are human and capable of experiencing any potential explosive emotions.

Sometimes the opposite of protest in the face of loss is over-isolation and withdrawal from the world around you. Of course, if you do that you will be at risk for grieving and not mourning.

Sad to say, some people around you will probably try to convince you that demonstrating any kind of emotional or spiritual protest is wrong. They may prematurely determine that you should just "accept" what has happened and "get on with your life." Yet, as you have come to realize, it is not that easy. So if and when you do show symptoms of protest, there are likely to be some people around you who may perceive you as being "out of control" or "not handling your grief" very well.

When you are protesting, people may get upset out of their own sense of helplessness. As already noted, the intensity of your own emotions may upset you (particularly if you grew up in a family where anger was seen as a bad emotion). Still, you must give yourself permission to feel whatever you feel and to express those feelings. Yes, any explosive emotions you may have do need to be expressed in healthy ways. That will not happen if you collaborate with well-intentioned but misinformed people who try to shut you down. If that happens, your body, mind, and spirit will likely be damaged in the process.

Watch out for people who may try to tell you that explosive emotions are not logical. "You being angry isn't going to change anything," they might say. You may be tempted to think from a rational perspective that they are right. That's just the problem— thinking is logical; feeling is not. Protest emotions are often an expression from the depth of your soul.

If explosive emotions are part of your journey (and they aren't for everyone), be aware that you have two avenues for expression—outward or inward. The outward avenue leads to healing; the inward does not. Keeping your explosive emotions inside can cause low self-esteem, depression, anxiety, guilt, physical complaints and sometimes even persistent thoughts of suicide. (Please see the important discussion of suicidal thoughts and feelings on p. 169.)

Explosive emotions are normal. However, they should soften in intensity and duration as you do the work of mourning. Again, I want to emphasize that the key is finding someone who will allow you to express any explosive emotions without inhibition or judgment, as long as you are not hurting yourself or anyone else, physically or emotionally. **Remember—you can't go around your grief or over it or under it— you must go through it.** I hope that as you journey through grief you will be surrounded by people who understand, support, and love you and will help you explore your explosive emotions without trying to stifle you.

A SURVIVOR SPEAKS

"I was really beyond mad at him for doing what he did. Sometimes I felt guilty about being angry, but I have learned to accept what I feel as being my real self. It really helped to find a support group where I found out other people have experienced the same thing. Once I learned it was okay to be mad at him, it has changed for me. I think I was protecting myself from my sadness by staying mad."

SELF-CARE SUGGESTIONS

Explosive emotions must be expressed, not repressed or, worse yet, totally denied. Don't expect or force yourself to have these feelings, but do be on the alert for them if they naturally arise. You will need a supportive listener who can tolerate, encourage, and validate your explosive emotions without judging, retaliating, or arguing with you. The comforting presence of someone who cares about you will help you seek self-understanding.

Be aware, though, of the difference between the right to feel explosive emotions and the right to act out these emotions in harmful ways. It's OK, sometimes even necessary, to feel angry. But if you hurt others or yourself or destroy property, the people who care about you will rightfully need to set limits on your behavior. Also, remind yourself that explosive emotions are usually masking underlying feelings of pain, helplessness, frustration, fear, and hurt. Befriend your explosive emotions and discover and embrace what's beneath them.

As you journey through your grief, continue to remind yourself that explosive emotions are not good or bad, right or wrong. They just are. They are your feelings, and they are symptoms of an injury that needs nurturing, not judging. Paradoxically, the way to diminish explosive emotions is to experience and express them, even when they feel irrational or overwhelming to you.

EXPRESS YOURSELF:
Go to *The Understanding Your Suicide Grief Journal* on pp. 92-93.

Guilt, Regret, Self-Blame, Shame, Embarrassment

This constellation of potential feeling may be a part of the emotional rollercoaster of your grief experience. Again, allow me to remind you—some of these feelings may apply to you while others may not. Also, a very important warning: Some people may project onto you that you SHOULD feel guilty. I've always found it interesting that we don't automatically prescribe guilt in other circumstances of death (cancer, accidents, etc.), yet I often hear people say to survivors of suicide, "I bet you feel guilty." Well, some survivors do, and some survivors don't, so we should not make this assumption.

Allow me to be very direct: You are not responsible for anyone's decision to die by suicide. The simple reality is that only one person is responsible: the person who died by suicide.

Sadly, our society tends to teach us that suicide is always caused by problems and that it is always someone's fault. The thought gets projected that the death was not beyond control. And yet– if your experience is anything like my experience with my friend Ken's death – if you could have prevented the death, you would have!

Yes, when someone you care about takes his or her own life, it's natural to think about actions you could or could not have taken to prevent the death. As one observer noted, "Human nature subconsciously resists so strongly the idea that we cannot control all the events of one's life that we would rather fault ourselves for a tragic occurrence than accept our inability to prevent it." In other words, we do not like acknowledging to ourselves that we are only human, so we blame ourselves instead. But of course, you are not to blame! Again, you are not to blame!

Yes, the tragic self-inflicted death of someone you care about invites you to explore your "if onlys" and "what ifs." Potential feelings of guilt, regret, and self-blame are only human, you are trying to go backward and control what you could not control. Still, some people may inappropriately encourage you to feel guilty, while others may try to quickly take any guilt or regret away from you. If you do express guilt or regret, someone might say to you, "There is nothing you could have done about it." (Essentially saying, "Don't feel what you are feeling.") In part, whether you actually could have prevented the suicide is not the point. The point is that you are feeling like you could have or should have and you need to express those feelings. If you find yourself expressing some "if onlys" and "what ifs," be compassionate with yourself. What a genuine and human response in the face of a suicide death.

I cannot emphasize enough that it will be vitally important to work through any and all aspects of guilt, regret, and self-blame you might have. Why? Because guilt can become a way of life built upon the belief of your own personal unworthiness. Then you risk becoming among the living dead. Because as long as you judge yourself as unworthy, you will never be able to fully integrate this grief into your life and discover renewed meaning and propose.

As long as you judge yourself as being guilty, you will feel shame. Shame is, in part, feeling sorry for who you are. Shame is a feeling that makes you want to avoid people and withdraw from the world around you. Shame can also make you want to keep the reality of a suicide death a secret. The problem with that is that secrecy feeds shame. After shame comes an unconscious tendency to self-punish.

So, at a time when you most need unconditional love and self-compassion, you may be at risk for personal abuse and self-neglect. In refusing to be self-compassionate, you could end up punishing yourself, living out your guilt, and creating the self-fulfilling prophecy of "getting what you deserve." Sadly, I have witnessed this unfolding process with way too many suicide loss survivors, and I don't want you to be one of them.

If you shroud the reality of this suicide death in secrecy, realize that where there is shame, there will be chronic pain. In effect, you will experience as much unhappiness and chronic sadness as you believe you deserve.

By being honest about the suicide and embracing the reality that only one person is responsible for the suicide (the person who died), the pain you feel can begin to soften. Opening yourself to any of your internalized shame, the pain and sadness you carry begin to soften and you discover you are no longer alone.

Some suicide loss survivors have taught me that intense feelings of embarrassment are a big part of their journey through grief. Embarrassment, a close cousin to shame, may result from imagined (and sometimes actual) gossip about the suicide among neighbors, faith groups, colleagues, and other social circles. Harbored embarrassment may make you feel that you owe an explanation to the curious who want to know what went wrong. You may fear that stories are being twisted and untruths told.

In truth, much of your embarrassment may be self-imposed. You are not responsible for the choice the person who died made, and the gossip-mongering you suppose may be taking place may not be happening at all. You also do not owe anyone an explanation, but you can set the tone for others by talking as openly and honestly as you can about the death. Just as your grief is natural, so is their curiosity and their concern for you. Keep in mind that they may simply be wondering what happened and how they can help you. Assume the best of others and you just might receive their best back.

THE DIFFERENCE BETWEEN BLAME AND RESPONSIBILITY

Yes, we loved and continue to love the person who has taken his or her own life. We are hesitant to place blame on this person. This begs for a distinction between blame and responsibility.

Whereas blame is anchored in accusation and judgment, responsibility is the acknowledgment of fact.

People who die by suicide do not deserve blame. However, they alone (even when the decision was complicated by tunnel vision and inability to see other choices) made a choice. Therefore, the responsibility is with them. To hold them responsible does not mean you love them any less.

The potential shame and embarrassment you are at risk for experiencing is naturally complex. Some of it has to do with how our society has viewed suicide over the years. There is still some legacy from the time when suicide was considered a crime and the person was forbidden a proper burial because taking one's life was considered a sin.

Despite the reality that there has been some movement away from official stigmatizing of suicide death (burial can occur in cemeteries like for everyone else; suicide is no longer considered a sin by most mainstream religions), as a survivor you will probably still experience some projected shame that comes from friends, neighbors, and other segments of society. Sadly, many people continue to make hurtful judgments about those who die by suicide and imply that something must be wrong in a family where suicide occurs.

Obviously, it is not only people from the outside who might make these judgments. Sometimes they come from within yourself, making your mourning more complicated. The potential result of external or internal shame is that you may tell yourself, "This is something I'm not going to talk about," which your emotions will translate into, "This is something I have to feel ashamed about." Then, you begin to hide feelings and keep secrets, which never works well. When the reality of suicide becomes unspeakable, your support system may begin to shut-down and feel like a pressure-cooker (see p. 66). The results of hiding, obscuring, or denying the truth are almost always worse than the feared responses when the truth is revealed. In addition, unless you acknowledge the reality openly and honestly, it is easy to feel entirely alone and isolated, as if no one has any idea what you are going through.

Guilt and its associated features can come in many ways, shapes, and forms. Additional aspects of this potential dimension of suicide grief include, but are not limited to, the following:

RELIEF-GUILT
Difficult for some survivors to express aloud is a felt sense of relief that may occur. This can naturally happen if you had a tumultuous relationship with lots of emotional ups and downs and/or previous suicide attempts. As one father said to me, "At least now I know where he is." This same father said to me, "How can I feel relief after he is dead?", reflecting this relief-guilt phenomenon. How very

human after experiencing the long, slow descent of someone you have loved to feel relieved that this long, winding road has come to an end. If you are feeling guilty about any feelings of relief, I urge you to find an understanding listener who can help you explore this part of your work of mourning.

MAGICAL THINKING AND GUILT

"I wish she would do it and get it over with," some people think when they are in a relationship with a chronically self-destructive person. Consciously or unconsciously, wishing for the death of someone—and then having that wish come true—can result in you feeling guilty. This is called "magical thinking" because, of course, your thoughts didn't cause the suicide death to take place.

Sometimes when the relationship has been difficult or constantly challenging, you may have had some direct thoughts about the relationship ending through death. Know that most all relationships have periods in which negative thoughts surface. But your mind does not have the power to inflict death. If you are in any way struggling with any of these kinds of thoughts, find someone to talk with who will be understanding, empathetic, and nonjudgmental.

GUILT AND ANGER

Some people have taught me that they experience feelings of guilt for being angry at the person who took his or her own life. "I love him, but I'm mad as hell at him... it is confusing to be mad one minute and guilty the next." Again, this calls out for you to find a trusted person or compassionate counselor to work through the naturalness of this phenomenon.

GUILT AND MEANS OF SUICIDE

This is when you may have done something like lend a gun to a friend for a supposed hunting expedition. Instead of going hunting, he used the gun on himself. Or, some families have always had guns around the house and now they experience guilt around that reality when a loved one dies by suicide with one of their own firearms.

I have also worked with some physicians who have unwittingly provided medication to someone, not realizing it was going to be used for a suicide. Again, if you are grieving this reality but not mourning it, find someone who can support and counsel you through this.

PARENTAL GUILT

If you are a parent of a child who has died by suicide, you may ask yourself, "Did I do something wrong? ... Did I not love them in a way they felt cared for and nurtured? ... If only we hadn't divorced maybe it would have made a difference!" These are but a few of the self-recriminations I have had parents express to me.

You may need a reminder that you loved your child. You were a good parent. You were not a perfect parent, but no one is. While you have had some influence over your child's life, you do not personally create every aspect of your child's way of being in the world. Our children are shaped and influenced by numerous factors beyond our control as parents. I should also note that in some situations, rationally or irrationally, some grieving parents blame their spouses/partners for some aspect of the suicide. If feelings of blame reside in you, talk compassionately (remembering his or her heart is also broken) to your spouse/partner about them and consider seeing a counselor together.

SPOUSAL/PARTNER GUILT

If you are a surviving spouse or partner, your grief experience may naturally be influenced by the stated or unstated contract you had to "look out for each other." Some of the potential vows we make at the time of marriage can give us a sense that we can always be there for one another. Yet, even the most caring spouse can sometimes feel very helpless in the face of something like a debilitating clinical depression. You may also be at risk for believing that others are silently blaming you, and, sad to say, some people around actually let it be known they do blame you. Not long before his death, my good friend Ken's lovely wife had decided, for some good reasons, to seek a divorce. Some people around her decided his death was then her fault. Nothing could have been further from the truth, yet some people must have a reason and this often means someone to blame! If this fits with any part of your experience, do not try to go it alone. Be self-compassionate and get support. You deserve it!

CHILD GUILT

I have had the honor of supporting young children, teens, and adult children who are suicide loss survivors of a parent. While there are unique developmental differences in perceptions surrounding issues of guilt, many of these children have taught me they feel they should have been able to prevent the suicide death of their parent. Some children feel they must have been unlovable or not good enough if a parent could take his or her own life. Others harbor secret feelings that their occasional, natural thoughts and/or acts of rebellion against their parent— "I hate you! I wish you were dead!"— contributed to the decision to suicide. For more information about talking to children about a suicide loss, see my book *Finding the Words: How to Talk with Children and Teens About Death, Suicide, Funerals, Homicide, Cremation, and Other End-of-Life Matters.*

Adult children may feel guilty if they had little contact with the parent before the death. The parent-child relationship is an extremely powerful one, and when the parent dies by suicide, the child may naturally feel many complicated feelings, including guilt. This is just one reason that child survivors of suicide often need special, focused care and companionship in the months and years after the suicide death of a parent.

MENTAL HEALTH CAREGIVER GUILT

Suicide deaths do take place in the lives of many mental health professionals. Despite one's best efforts to assess for suicide risk and to try to help a client "choose life," it can be devastating when someone you have tried to help dies by suicide. Fortunately, there is a resource for mental health care providers who have experienced the death of a client to suicide. Go to the website at https://www.cliniciansurvivor.org.

JOY-GUILT

Like relief-guilt, joy-guilt is about thinking that happy feelings are bad at a time of grief and loss. Experiencing any kind of joy after a suicide death may leave you feeling guilty. One day you will find yourself smiling or laughing at something, only to potentially chastise yourself for having felt happy for even a passing moment.

It's as if your loyalty to the person who took his or her own life demands that you be sad all the time now that they are gone. That is certainly not true of course. As you do the work of mourning, your natural healing journey will allow you to start experiencing more and more happiness and joy and less and less pain. Change and movement surrounding these emotions is obviously a good thing.

Whatever you do, do not self-punish yourself for any feelings of happiness and joy you may experience! If you are feeling guilty about having this kind of experience, find someone to talk to about it.

LONGSTANDING PERSONALITY FACTORS

Some people have felt guilty their entire lives. I hope you are not one of them, but you may be. Why? Because some people learn early in life, typically during childhood, that they are responsible when something sad or hurtful happens. When someone dies by suicide, it is one more thing to feel guilty about. If all-encompassing guilt is part of your experience, seek out a professional counselor who can help you work on understanding the nature and extent of your feelings.

Whatever your unique feelings related to any guilt, regret, self-blame, shame or embarrassment, don't let them go unexpressed. They may be a natural part of your journey, and like all dimensions of grief, they need to be explored. So, don't try to make this journey

A SURVIVOR SPEAKS

"I think I knew he was depressed, but I didn't make him get help. I tried a couple of times... but sometimes I say 'if only' to myself. At first, I kept these 'if onlys' to myself, but I have discovered since then that I had to get them out. I have found some caring people who really seem to understand my need to review my 'if onlys.'"

alone! Find compassionate people who will walk with you and listen to you without judgment.

SELF-CARE SUGGESTIONS

If any aspect of guilt, regret, self-blame, shame, or embarrassment is a part of your experience, look for a compassionate, patient, and non-judgmental listener. If you feel it, acknowledge it and express it openly.

Don't allow others to prescribe these feeling to you if they are not part of your journey. Be on the alert for those people who project onto you that you *should* feel guilty. Also, be careful not to assume people are silently blaming you for the death. I have had a number of survivors teach me that they fear that other people will see them as failures because of the suicide. While a few misinformed people might believe or even say this, most people, particularly compassionate people, will not. Sometimes I have found this is a projection from within yourself. So, do not assume that everyone around you perceives you as a failure and believes you should have been able to prevent the suicide.

On the other hand, don't allow others to explain your feelings away. While they may try to help you, this attitude will not allow you to talk out what you think and feel on the inside. When you explore any feelings of guilt, regret, or self-blame, you will usually come to understand the limits of any sense of personal responsibility.

As you express yourself, remember—you aren't perfect. No one is. Something tragic happened that you wish had not. Someone you cared about has died by suicide. At times, you will naturally go back and review if you could have said or done anything to change this painful reality. Allow yourself this review time, but as you do so, be compassionate with yourself. Continue to remind yourself that there are some things in life you cannot change, but that even if you could have done things differently, it may not have necessarily changed what occurred.

One of the worst things you could do is to ignore or repress any of these kinds of feelings you might have. Many physical and emotional problems may result if you try to push these feelings away without giving them the attention they deserve. Remember, as previously noted, secrecy feeds shame. After shame then comes an unconscious tendency to self-punish, and that is often accompanied by retreating from the world around you. I don't want that for you. Instead, I want you to mourn openly and honestly so you can go on to live fully until you die. That is the best legacy you can leave both those who went before you and those who remain after you—to live fully until you die. Again, to do that requires that you mourn fully while you are alive. If any of the feelings I explored with you in this section are trying to get your attention, muster up the courage to go see a caring grief-informed counselor who has the sensitivity to walk with you on this painful journey.

EXPRESS YOURSELF:
Go to *The Understanding Your Suicide Grief Journal* on pp. 94-97.

Sadness, Depression, Loneliness, Vulnerability

Some of the most natural aspects of grief following suicide are sadness, depression, loneliness, and vulnerability. Yes, these are natural, authentic emotions after the sudden death of someone you care about. Of course you are sad. Of course you feel deep sorrow. Allowing yourself to feel your sadness is in large part what your journey toward healing is all about. I suggest you say out loud, "I have every right to feel sad, depressed, lonely, and vulnerable!"

Naturally, you don't like feeling sad, depressed, lonely, or vulnerable. These experiences sap pleasure from your life, yet to experience these emotions is so very human. Experiencing them is not a judgment about your ability to cope. You need not feel ashamed of these feelings if they apply to you. After all, they are encountered by most everyone who is a survivor of someone who has died by suicide.

These emotions are often experienced in a series of rollercoaster cycles, sometimes up, sometimes down. One day may seem survivable and hopeful; the next day you are caught in an overwhelming wave of deep sadness. As life goes forward, you may feel incredibly vulnerable.

Weeks, or often months, will pass before you are fully confronted by the depths of your sorrow. The slow-growing nature of this is appropriate. You could not and should not try to tolerate all of your sadness at once. Your body, mind, and spirit need time to work together to embrace the depth of your loss. Please be patient with yourself.

You also have the right to feel alone in the world despite the fact that you may be surrounded by people who care about you. Hand in hand with feeling alone comes a sense of vulnerability. Vulnerability relates to the attitudes and feelings you have when confronted with the reality of a suicide death. It is often a time of constant ups and downs, a time of a multitude of emotions and disorganized and confused thinking. You may feel uncertain about yourself and your future. It can seem as if you have lost your way in the midst of the wilderness. You might feel dazed, unable to focus. You may feel fragile and on edge.

Obviously, I have emphasized throughout this book the theme of being with your feelings as this journey unfolds. If you feel the vulnerability I described above, I ask you not to think of it as "bad"

THE DARK NIGHT OF THE SOUL

While grief affects all aspects of your life—your physical, cognitive, emotional, social, and spiritual selves—it is fundamentally a spiritual journey.

In grief, your understanding of who you are, why you are here, and whether or not life is worth living is challenged. A significant loss plunges you into what C.S. Lewis, Eckhart Tolle, and various authors have called "the dark night of the soul." Life may suddenly seem meaningless. Nothing makes sense. Everything you believed and held dear may have been turned upside-down. The structure of your world might seem to have collapsed.

The dark night of the soul can be a long and very black night indeed. It is uncomfortable and scary. The pain of that place can seem intolerable, and yet the only way to emerge into the light of a new morning is to experience the night.

I often note that one of the main paradoxes of grief is that you must make friends with the darkness before you can enter the light. The natural sadness and depression of your grief live in that darkness. Be present to them in doses. Sit with them, get to know them, and express them outside of yourself. The more you allow yourself to feel and attend to your natural sadness, the more momentum you will gain on your journey toward healing.

and "avoidable." Traumatic grief brings times of vulnerability. And, at a fundamental level, vulnerability is part of being human. Some things that come along in life are more powerful than we are. They leave us feeling defenseless in ways we may have never imagined. You feel totally naked emotionally, and this feeling is not something you can simply push aside.

This is a time of many changes and instability. You are in what is called "liminal space." *Limina* is the Latin word for threshold, the space betwixt and between. Liminal space is that spiritual place you hate to be, but where the experience of suicide grief often takes you. Yes, you feel because you are alive and human. Paradoxically, an appropriate way to cope with your vulnerability is to embrace it. In other words, honor this time of extreme tenderness in your life. Think of it as a season in your life that will not last forever. Sometimes we want to rush to the next season (often from winter to spring), yet we must still endure the cold and uncomfortable for a while. You will also find guidelines for helping you with your vulnerability in Touchstone Seven, Nurture Yourself, and Touchstone Eight, Reach Out for Help.

Now, let's return to the exploration of sadness and depression that often accompanies loneliness and newfound vulnerability. You may find that certain times and circumstances bring overwhelming feelings of grief. Sometimes something as simple as a sound (a car starting up, a song), a smell (a favorite food, a perfume or cologne), a sight (a car similar to the one he or she used to drive, watching a lovely sunset), a touch (a fabric that reminds you of a connection to the person). Some people find that weekends, holidays, family meals, or any kind of anniversary occasion can be hard, as can bedtime, waking up in the middle of the night, and arriving home to an empty house. These natural "griefbursts" (see p. 165) can bring huge waves, sometimes tidal waves, of sadness. Allow yourself to experience these feelings without shame or self-judgment, no matter where and when they occur. When these waves come, you may find it helpful to reach out to a trusted friend and share the experience, or befriend your feelings and then gently move forward with your day.

Do be on alert for some people around you who might think you should be able to control or subdue your feelings of sadness. Nothing could be further from the truth. Your sadness is a symptom of your wound. Just as physical wounds require attention, so do emotional wounds.

Sometimes your feelings of sadness and sorrow can be overwhelming enough to be classified as clinical depression. After all, the mourning that comes with a suicide death can share many symptoms with depression, including sleep disturbances, appetite changes, decreased energy, withdrawal, guilt, dependency, lack of concentration, and a sense of loss of control. You may have a hard time functioning at home and at work, which may compound your feelings of isolation, helplessness, and vulnerability.

You are probably aware that your physical body is separate from, but interconnected with, your mind and emotions. Many of the suicide loss survivors I have had the honor of supporting have reported multiple physical symptoms in the weeks and months following the death. Severe physical symptoms can be brought on by your emotional and spiritual response to the death. It is very real and does not mean you are a hypochondriac! The overwhelming grief that suicide unfolds can result in very intense physical reactions.

The onset of depression can also upset and affect the healthy chemical balance of your body. If you stay in a depressed state for a long period of time without any relief, your body may either be depleted of or overproduce chemicals that can keep you stuck in your depression. When this happens, a cycle has started in which your emotional/spiritual depression now involves the body as well.

Think of it this way: If you are physically ill with the flu, you eventually feel emotionally wiped out as well. Even though things may be fine in your life while you have the flu, staying in bed for a few days can make you feel depressed. So remember, mind and body interact; they influence each other. **If you are feeling totally immobilized by depression, please get some help from a grief-informed counselor immediately.**

Fortunately, many physicians and mental-health care providers are learning to prescribe anti-depressants more wisely. Specifically, they are learning how to do what is called a "differential diagnosis" between normal sadness with depressive features in contrast to a clinical depression. If you're unsure about the distinction between normal sadness and clinical depression, see the additional information titled "Normal Grief or Clinical Depression?" on the next page.

Thoughts of suicide may enter your own mind during your grief journey. The suicide of someone in your life has made the very idea of suicide more real to you. However, that certainly does not mean you should do it. You have other choices, like getting help immediately, if you have any concerns about this at all.

Yes, I have had suicide loss survivors say things to me like, "I wouldn't mind if I didn't wake up tomorrow." Comments like this reflect a need to further explore the depth of your sadness. It's natural to experience these passive thoughts; however, it is not natural to want to or make plans to take your own life when someone in your life has died by suicide!

Again, if you have been thinking of taking your own life, get help right now from a professional caregiver. I also ask you to remember that the very fact that you are reading this book demonstrates that your desire to mourn and to integrate this death into your life far outweighs any desire you might have to end your life. Yes, you have been torn apart and you are in deep pain. But to help your injury heal, you must openly acknowledge what the life and death of the person who has died has meant to you.

NORMAL GRIEF OR CLINICAL DEPRESSION?

For centuries, most people viewed depression as a sign of physical or mental weakness, not as a real health problem. But today, clinical depression is recognized as a common health challenge with a biological basis that is often exacerbated by psychological and social stress. In fact, each year about ten percent of American adults experience some form of clinical depression.

There are a number of influences that can play a role in the development of depression, including genetics, stress, and changes in body and brain function. Many people with clinical depression have abnormally low levels of certain brain chemicals and slowed cellular activity in areas of the brain that control mood, appetite, sleep, and other functions.

Clinical depression affects not only your mood but also how you think about things, making your thoughts more negative and pessimistic. It affects how you feel about yourself, lowering your sense of self-worth. It impacts how you act, often making you more ambivalent or disinterested in life and can make you easily upset about even minor things.

Everyone experiences times of sadness in response to the stresses and losses of life. The feelings that go along with these stressful events are naturally unpleasant. Yet the occasional sadness that we all sometimes feel because of life's disappointments and stresses is very different from clinical depression. Unlike normal feelings of sadness and loss, clinical depression can be debilitating.

In many ways, depression and grief are similar. Common shared symptoms are feelings of sadness, lack of interest in usually pleasurable activities, and problems with eating and sleeping. The central difference is that while grief is a normal, natural, and healthy process, clinical depression is not.

One area to pay particular attention to is feelings of self-worth. While people who are grieving a death often feel guilty over some aspect of the relationship or the circumstances of the death, they do not typically feel worthless. In other words, people with grief depression may feel guilty and even hopeless for a time, while people with clinical depression often feel a generalized sense of low self-worth and hopelessness.

NORMAL GRIEF	CLINICAL DEPRESSION
You have normal grief if you...	You may be clinically depressed if you...
○ respond to comfort and support.	○ do not accept support.
○ are capable of being openly angry.	○ are irritable and complain but do not directly express anger.
○ relate your depressed feelings to the loss experience.	○ do not relate your feelings of depression to a particular life event.
○ can still experience moments of enjoyment in life.	○ exhibit an all-pervading sense of gloom.
○ exhibit feelings of sadness and emptiness.	○ project a sense of hopelessness and chronic emptiness.
○ may have transient physical complaints.	○ have chronic physical complaints.
○ express guilt over some specific aspect of the loss.	○ have generalized feelings of guilt.
○ feel a temporary loss of self-esteem.	○ feel a deep and ongoing loss of self-esteem.

The difference between the normal sadness of grief and clinical depression can also be measured by how long the feelings last and to what extent your daily activities are impaired. Grief softens over time; clinical depression does not. After the numbing and chaotic early days and weeks of grief, your daily schedule begins to proceed as usual. If you are clinically depressed, you may be unable to function day-to-day.

Depression can complicate grief in two ways. It can create short-term symptoms that are more severe and debilitating than those normally associated with grief. In addition, clinical depression can cause symptoms of grief to persist longer than normal and potentially worsen. (Continued on next page.)

If you or someone who cares about you thinks you may be clinically depressed, I invite you to review the chart on the previous page and make a checkmark next to any symptoms you think apply to you. If you place checkmarks in the clinical depression column, that means it's time to see your primary-care provider or a counselor. They will help you discern what's going on and get you the extra care you need. Remember—getting help is not a sign of weakness; it is a sign of strength.

The good news is that clinical depression is treatable. With appropriate assessment and treatment, most people with clinical depression find significant relief. Untreated depression, on the other hand, can raise your risk for a number of additional health problems. It will also prevent you from moving forward in your journey through grief. You deserve to get help so you can continue to mourn in ways that help you heal.

SELF-CARE SUGGESTIONS

As you embrace any and all feelings of sadness, depression, loneliness, and vulnerability, you will need the comfort of trusted people—close friends, loving family members, and sometimes compassionate professional caregivers. Your feelings of sadness can leave you feeling isolated, alone, and vulnerable. I want you to be on the watch for the symptoms I have outlined related to clinical depression and urge you to immediately seek professional help if you have any concerns at all. Again, depression is something help is available for. **Do not suffer alone and in silence!**

Now, allow me to provide you with some general principles of self-care that can help you learn not to fight these kinds of feelings, but to befriend them. Paradoxically, the only way to eventually lessen your pain is to move toward it, not away from it. Moving toward your sadness is not always an easy thing to do. Sometimes when you admit to feeling sad and sorrowful, or deeply depressed, people who think they are helping you say things like, "Now, you just need to look at the good in your life," or "You being sad isn't going to do anybody any good," or, worse yet, "You just need to snap out of it!" Comments like this hinder, not help you, on your pathway to integrating this overwhelming loss into your life.

To be able to move toward these emotions requires that you find and make use of compassionate people with whom you can express your authentic feelings. If you are using this book in concert with a counseling or support group experience, odds are good that you have found just that!

Talk openly about where you see yourself surrounding these feelings outlined above. You need people to affirm and support you right now. As you journey through the wilderness of your grief, you need people who will walk with you – not behind or in front of you, but beside you.

If talking is an avenue that works for you, keep talking until you have exhausted your capacity to talk. Doing so will help reconnect you to the world outside of yourself. Or, if you can't talk it out, write it out! Paint it out! Sing it out! But get the feelings outside of yourself. And, if fitting with your personality, give yourself permission to cry—as often and as much as you need to. Tears can help cleanse you body, mind, and spirit.

Allowing yourself to spend some time alone after a significant loss in your life is an essential self-nurturing practice. It affords you the opportunity to be unaffected by others' wants and needs. Spending

A SURVIVOR SPEAKS

"I felt so sad, depressed, and alone. But, here is the good news, I reached out and got the help I needed. No one should try to go through the pain of the death of someone to suicide alone. Please get help. I did, and it has been my lifeline."

time alone allows for reflection, introspection, and development of your inner self. **Alone time does not mean you are being selfish. Instead, you will experience rest and renewal in ways you otherwise would not.**

Allow me to also remind you that these feelings of sadness, depression, loneliness, and vulnerability do, in fact, have some value in your grief journey. Actually, these feelings are trying to help you slow down while you work to heal the wounds of your grief. It may seem strange, yet depression often slows down your body and prevents major organ systems from being damaged. Depression also allows you to turn inward and slow down your spirit. It aids in your healing and provides time to slowly begin reordering your life. These natural feelings can ultimately help you to assess old ways of being, look at how you've been changed by this experience, and make plans for the future.

A warning: Giving attention to, experiencing, and honoring these feelings of sadness, depression, loneliness, and vulnerability should help them soften over time. Remember that fancy-sounding word *perturbation* I introduced in the beginning of this chapter? I would gently remind you that it means "the capacity to experience change and movement." If you feel *stuck* and have not reached out for help, you can read as many books as you want, but you may not feel like you are experiencing the "change and movement" you need and deserve. So, don't be your own worst enemy. Care enough about yourself to get the kind of support and understanding that will help you see an eventual softening in your journey. Do your work of authentic mourning, renew your divine spark, live your life deeply and eventually reach out and re-engage in the world around you!

EXPRESS YOURSELF:
Go to *The Understanding Your Suicide Grief Journal* on pp. 98-100.

Relief, Release

While I introduced this potential dimension of response under relief-guilt, p. 112, it deserves some additional attention in its own right. Some suicide loss survivors have taught me they sometimes feel a sense of relief and release after the death. Perhaps the person had suffered a long, debilitating decline over many years. Some people have been in mourning for a "lost person" long before the suicide occurs. Your relief, then, is natural and normal. Understand that your relief does not equate to a lack of concern or love for the person who is no longer here.

A SURVIVOR SPEAKS

"My relationship with him had more downs than ups. He had some great qualities but living with him was so draining. I never knew what to expect next. I know it may not sound right, but sometimes I'm just really glad my life is in a much better place than it was before he took his life. Relief—yes, I can relate to that!"

When someone who abused you dies by suicide (physically, sexually, emotionally), you may feel a sense of relief that equates with a feeling of being safe for the first time. This is normal and appropriate. Obviously, this kind of history connected to the relationship calls out to you to go backward and review the history of abuse as part of your eventual healing. Do not try to do this kind of grief work alone. This often calls for a caring professional caregiver who knows how to gently support you in your healing process.

When appropriate, allowing yourself to acknowledge any aspects of relief as part of your grief experience can be a critical step in your journey. Whatever your feelings, working to embrace them creates the opportunity to find hope in your healing.

SELF-CARE SUGGESTIONS

If you feel a sense of relief or release, write about it, or better yet, talk about it. Find someone you trust who will listen to you, really hear you, and in no way sit in judgment of what you are experiencing. If you feel guilty about being relieved, talk about it with someone who can help you feel understood and sort out the naturalness of your sense of relief. Remember—relief does not equal a lack of concern or love for the person who is now dead. Whatever you do, don't deny feelings of relief if you have them. They deserve to be honored just like any other of the feelings you might have!

EXPRESS YOURSELF:
Go to *The Understanding Your Suicide Grief Journal* on p. 101.

A Final Thought about the Feelings You May Experience

When you add up all the thoughts and feelings you've had since this death—as well as all the emotions you're yet to have in the months to come—we call this experience "grief." It's a deceptively small, simple word for such a wide-ranging, challenging assortment of feelings.

The ways you behave when you're having these feelings is also part of your grief journey. Mourning—or expressing your feelings outside of yourself—is sometimes, but not always, intentional. Your feelings may come out in strange and unpredictable ways, and this, too, is normal.

I hope you will be kind to yourself as you encounter and befriend all your grief thoughts, feelings, and behaviors. Patience is paramount, as is self-compassion. You feel what you feel; there are no rights or wrongs. And when you're struggling with your feelings or need to let them out, I hope you'll remember to reach out to the people who care about you. Experiencing the feelings is normal and necessary, but so is expressing them outside of yourself and having them affirmed by others.

This is the cycle of experiencing a feeling in grief: feel it, acknowledge it, befriend it, share it, and finally, have it witnessed and empathized with by others. Repeat. Each time you complete the circle, you are taking one small step toward integrating this loss into your life.

TOUCHSTONE FIVE

Understand the
Six Needs of Mourning

If you are looking for a detailed map for your journey through suicide grief, none exists. Your wilderness is an undiscovered wilderness and you its first explorer.

But those of us who have experienced a death of someone to suicide have found that our paths have many similarities. A number of authors have proposed models of grief that refer to "stages." As I suggested in Touchstone Two about grief misconceptions, we do not go through orderly, predictable stages of grief, with clear-cut beginnings and endings.

> "I knew that running from the darkness would only lead to greater darkness later on. I learned to live and mourn simultaneously."
>
> Gerald L. Sittser

Still, when we are mourning a death to suicide, we do have some similar needs. Instead of referring to stages of grief, I say that we as mourners have six central needs. Remember I said in the Introduction that as we journey through grief, we need to follow the trail markers, or the touchstones, if we are to find our way out of the wilderness? The trail marker we will discuss in this chapter defines the six central needs of mourning. Perhaps you can think of Touchstone Five as its own little grouping of trail markers.

The six needs of mourning aren't orderly or predictable. Though I've numbered them for easy reference, they aren't really sequential. You will probably jump around in random fashion as you work on these six needs of mourning. You will address each need when you are ready to do so. And sometimes you will be working on more than one need at a time.

You will find that several of the six needs of mourning reiterate and reinforce concepts found in other touchstones of this book. I hope this reinforcement helps you embrace how very important these fundamental concepts are.

What's more, your awareness of these needs will help you take a participative, action-oriented approach to healing in grief as opposed to thinking of grief as something you passively experience. You'll recall in Touchstone Two that we reviewed the important distinction between grief and mourning. Grief is what you think and feel on the inside; mourning is when you express those thoughts and feelings outside of yourself. These are not called the six needs of grief but rather the six needs of mourning. Why? Because while you will naturally experience all of them internally, to integrate them into your life, you will also need to intentionally, proactively engage with all of them externally as well.

Grief is the noun; mourning is the verb.

Grief is the vehicle; mourning is the engine.

Grief is the rock; mourning is the catapult.

THE SIX NEEDS OF MOURNING

1. Acknowledge the reality of the death.

2. Embrace the pain of the loss.

3. Remember the person who died.

4. Develop a new self-identity.

5. Search for meaning.

6. Let others help you— now and always.

The reality is that the six needs of mourning, while painful and difficult, are also, over time, transformative. They will carry you through the wilderness of your grief. They'll help give you the momentum you need to not only survive but eventually thrive again.

MOURNING NEED 1:

Acknowledge the Reality of the Death

You can know something in your head but not in your heart. This is what often happens when someone you love dies by suicide. This first need of mourning, a close cousin to Touchstone One (Open to the Presence of Your Loss), involves gently confronting the reality that someone you care about will never physically come back into your life again.

Because the nature of a suicide death is sudden, and naturally traumatic, acknowledging the full reality usually doesn't happen in days, but in weeks, even months, and sometimes years. **To survive you will probably naturally need to push away the reality of the death at times.** But as I have tried to gently convey throughout this book, embracing this kind of painful reality is never quick, easy, or efficient. You may find it helpful to consider re-reading the section in Touchstone Three, pages 64-68, where I outlined the circumstances that often accompany suicide. This can help you see how your unique circumstances have a natural influence on this need to acknowledge the reality of the death.

A SURVIVOR SPEAKS

"I kept fading in and out from the reality of what happened. At times I just kept thinking it was a bad dream. But it wasn't, and slowly I allowed myself to realize it really happened."

You may move back and forth between protesting and encountering the reality of the death. You may discover yourself replaying events surrounding the death and confronting memories, both good and bad. This replay is a vital part of this need of mourning. It's as if each time you talk it out, the event is a little more real.

One moment the reality of the loss may be tolerable; another moment it may be unbearable. Be patient with this need. At times, you may feel like running away and hiding. At other times, you may hope you will awaken from what seems like a bad dream or nightmare. As you express what you think and feel outside of yourself, you will be working on this important need.

Remember—this first need of mourning, like the other five that follow, may intermittently require your attention long into the future. Be patient and compassionate with yourself as you work on each of them.

EXPRESS YOURSELF:
Go to *The Understanding Your Suicide Grief Journal* on pp. 104-105.

MOURNING NEED 2:

Embrace the Pain of the Loss

Like Touchstone One (Open to the Presence of Your Loss), this need of mourning requires us to embrace the pain of our loss— something we don't instinctively want to do. It is easier to avoid, repress, or deny the pain of grief than it is to confront it, yet it is in confronting our pain that we learn to reconcile ourselves to it.

In the grief-caregiver training courses I teach, my students often ask me what I mean by "embracing" the pain of grief. I also like to use the verb "befriending," and people ask about that term as well.

When I say that this need of mourning is to embrace your pain, I'm first asking you to acknowledge the appropriateness of the pain. Someone you love—someone who gave your life meaning—has died. Of course it hurts! Of course you feel pain! Where there was love or attachment, there will naturally be pain when a relationship is severed by death.

But in addition to emphasizing that you must recognize your pain as normal, I'm further suggesting that over time you even need to learn to look upon your pain as part of your love and make it your friend. **As you probably realize, love and grief are two sides of the same precious coin. If your love is good and valuable, so, too, is your grief.** And like your love, it will require your loving attention in the months and years to come.

Even so, you will probably discover that you need to dose yourself in embracing your pain. In other words, you cannot (nor should you try to) overload yourself with the hurt all at one time. Sometimes you may need to distract yourself from the pain of the death, while at other times you will need to create a safe place to move toward it.

Feeling your pain can sometimes zap you of your energy. When your energy is low, you may be tempted to suppress your grief or even run from it. If you start running and keep running, you may never heal. Dose your pain: yes! Deny your pain: no!

Unfortunately, as I have said, our culture tends to encourage the denial of pain. We misunderstand the role of hurt, pain, and suffering. If you openly express your feelings of grief, misinformed friends may advise you to "carry on" or "keep your chin up." If, on the other hand, you remain "strong" and "in control," you may be congratulated for "doing well" with your grief. Actually, doing well with your grief means becoming well acquainted with your pain. Don't let others deny you this critical mourning need.

Embracing the pain of grief is a vital part of active, authentic mourning. You will befriend your pain by sitting with it, being present to it, thinking about it, and feeling it. But to convert grief into mourning, you must also express it outside of yourself regularly.

Cry if you feel like crying, and let your tears be seen and heard by people who care about you. Tell your friends and family what you are thinking and feeling. Describe your pain to them. People who listen without judgment are your most important helpers as you work on this mourning need. As you encounter your pain, you will also need to nurture yourself in all the ways we will discuss in Touchstone Seven.

A SURVIVOR SPEAKS

"I like the idea of dosing my pain from this excruciating loss. If I tried to do this quickly, I would find it impossible. Dr. Wolfelt helped me remember: Go slowly! There are no rewards for speed!"

Never forget that grief requires convalescence: something that by its nature is slow and recursive. Your pain will probably ebb and flow for months, even years; embracing it when it washes over you will require patience, support, and strength.

EXPRESS YOURSELF:
Go to *The Understanding Your Suicide Grief Journal* on pp. 106-107.

MOURNING NEED 3:

Remember the Person Who Died

Do you have any kind of relationship with people after they die? Of course. You have a relationship of memory. Precious memories, dreams reflecting the significance of the relationship, and objects that link you to the person who died (such as photos, souvenirs, clothing, etc.) are examples of some of the things that give testimony to a different form of a continued relationship. This need of mourning involves allowing and encouraging yourself to pursue this relationship.

The process of beginning to embrace your memories often begins with the funeral. The ceremony offers you an opportunity to remember the person who died and helps to affirm the value of the life that was lived. The memories you embrace during the time of the funeral set the tone for the changed nature of the relationship. Even later on, meaningful ceremonies encourage the expression of cherished memories and allow for both tears and laughter in the company of others who loved the person who died by suicide.

Embracing your memories can be a very slow and, at times, painful process that occurs in small steps. Remember—don't try to do all your work of mourning at once. Go slowly and be patient with yourself. This memory work is often naturally complicated when it follows a death to suicide. But you can and will be able to do it at your own pace and in your own time.

ON GOING BACKWARD BEFORE YOU CAN GO FORWARD

Our culture may be encouraging you to move on, but one of the paradoxes of grief is that you have to go backward before you can go forward. This is particularly true with a suicide death.

Grief by its very nature is a recursive process. That means it curves and spirals back on itself. It's repetitive. It covers the same ground more than once. Often it's not even a two-steps-forward, one-step-backward kind of journey. Instead, it can be a one-step-forward, two-steps-in-a-circle, one-step-backward process. It takes time, patience, and yes, lots of backward motion before forward motion predominates.

When you actively remember the person who died, you go backward. When you tell the story of your love and loss from the beginning, you go backward. When you think back to earlier losses in your life and how they may be affecting your current grief, you go backward. When you work on your self-identity and think back to old interests you may now want to revisit, you go backward. These and other backward-looking activities are a normal and necessary part of grief.

So by all means, go backward as much and as often as you need to. As long as you are actively engaging with your grief, you can trust that one day you will look up and find that you have indeed moved forward in meaningful ways.

Some people may try to take your memories away. Trying to be helpful, they encourage you to take down photos of the person who died. They may tell you to keep busy or that you'd be better off to move out of your house. You, too, may think avoiding memories would be better for you. And why not? You are living in a culture that teaches you to move away from your grief, instead of toward it.

Following are a few examples of things you can do to keep memories alive while embracing the reality that the person has died:

- Talking out or writing down favorite memories.
- Giving yourself permission to keep some special keepsakes or "linking objects" (see p. 168).
- Displaying photos of the person who is now dead.
- Visiting places of special significance that stimulate memories of times shared together.
- Reviewing photo albums at special times such as holidays, birthdays, and anniversaries.

Perhaps one of the best ways to embrace memories is through creating a "memory book" that contains special photographs you have selected and perhaps other memorabilia such as ticket stubs, menus, etc. Organize these items, place them in an album, and write out the memories reflected in the photos. This book can then become a valued collection of memories that you can review whenever you so desire.

The act of creating a memory book is mourning. Showing it to others and talking about it is, too. Of course, you don't need a memory book to share your memories. You can simply sit down with a friend and talk about them or attend a support group that allows you to do the same.

I also need to mention here the reality that memories are not always pleasant. If this applies to you, addressing this need of mourning can be even more difficult. To ignore painful or ambivalent memories is to prevent yourself from living fully for the rest of your life. You will need someone who can nonjudgmentally explore any painful memories with you. If you repress or deny these memories, you risk carrying an underlying sadness or anger into your future. If your memories are particularly challenging or traumatic, I urge you to see a counselor who is trained to help you with memory work.

When people share their fond memories of the person who died with you, this can be a great gift. Welcome and cherish these new stories and add them to your storehouse of treasures. Yet I also know that sometimes others may share memories and information with you that are not so pleasant. Many mourners have told me that only after a death did they learn surprising or disturbing secrets about someone who died. These revelations can be exceptionally hard to integrate into your understanding of the person's life, especially since the person is no longer here to discuss them with. If this happens to you and you are having trouble coming to terms with new information, I urge you to see a counselor for a few sessions. A skilled, compassionate professional will be able to help you through this understandably confusing time.

A SURVIVOR SPEAKS

"There were some great times and there were some really bad times. I found out I had to work with both the good memories and the bad. I also had to mourn for so much of what I wish could have been."

In general, however, remembering the past makes hoping for the future possible. Your future will become open to new experiences only to the extent that you embrace the past. I often say: You must listen to the music of the past, so you can sing in the present, and dance into the future.

EXPRESS YOURSELF:
Go to *The Understanding Your Suicide Grief Journal* on pp. 108-115.

MOURNING NEED 4:

Develop a New Self-Identity

Your personal identity, or self-perception, is the result of the ongoing process of establishing a sense of who you are. Part of your self-identity comes from the relationships you have with other people. When someone with whom you have a relationship dies, your self-identity, or the way you see yourself, naturally changes.

You may have gone from being a "wife" or "husband" to a "widow" or "widower." You may have gone from being a "parent" to a "bereaved parent." The way you define yourself and the way society defines you is changed. As one woman said, "I used to have a husband and was part of a couple. Now I'm not only single, but a single parent and a widow... I hate that word. It makes me sound like a lonely spider."

A death often requires you to take on new roles that had been filled by the person who died. After all, someone still has to take out the garbage, buy the groceries, and make the Wi-Fi work. You confront your changed identity every time you do something that used to be done by the person who died. This can be very hard work and, at times, can leave you feeling very drained of emotional, physical, and spiritual energy.

You may occasionally feel child-like as you struggle with your changing identity. You may feel a temporarily heightened dependence on others as well as feelings of helplessness, frustration, inadequacy, and fear. These feelings can be overwhelming and scary, but they are actually a natural response to this important need of mourning.

As you give attention to this need, be certain to keep other major changes to a minimum if at all possible. Now is not the time for a major move or taking on new responsibilities. Your energy is already depleted. Don't deplete it even more by making significant changes and taking on too many tasks.

Remember—do what you need to do in order to survive as you try to re-anchor yourself. To be temporarily dependent on others as you struggle with a changed identity does not make you weak, bad, or inferior. Your self-identity has been assaulted. Be compassionate with yourself. Accept the support of others.

Many people discover that as they work on this need, they ultimately discover some positive aspects of their changed self-identity. You may develop a renewed confidence in yourself. You might reveal a more caring, kind, and sensitive part of yourself. You may develop an assertive part of your identity that empowers you to go on living even though you continue to feel a sense of loss. (To learn more about the self-identity changes that come with grief, see Touchstone Ten.)

A SURVIVOR SPEAKS

"It took me some time to figure out who I would be without her. I'd always been a husband, now I was a widower and a survivor of a suicide death. Wow—that was so much for me to take in. So I'm glad I had the support group friends who helped me with this."

EXPRESS YOURSELF:
Go to *The Understanding Your Suicide Grief Journal* on pp. 116-118.

MOURNING NEED 5:

Search for Meaning

When someone you love takes his or her own life, you naturally question the meaning and purpose of life. You probably will question your philosophy of life and explore religious and spiritual values as you work on this need. You may discover yourself searching for meaning in your continued living as you ask "Why?" and "How?" questions. "Why did this happen now, in this way?" "How could God let this happen?" The death reminds you of your lack of control. It can leave you feeling powerless.

As Edward K. Rynearson wisely noted following his wife Julie's death to suicide, "While religious or spiritual concepts might have prepared me for Julie's death, they could not prepare me for her violent dying. There is no spiritual belief or religion, despite any scripture or hymn or sermon, that finds order or meaning in a violent death." Yes, as he discovered, suicide can naturally complicate this search for meaning need. It can throw your spiritual/religious/philosophical life into disarray. It naturally disrupts any kind of spiritual rhythm you may have been experiencing in your life. So, I plead with you: Be patient with yourself and repeat the mantra "No rewards for speed!"

After all, the person who died was a part of you. This death means you mourn a loss not only outside of yourself, but inside of yourself as well. At times, overwhelming sadness and loneliness may be your constant companions. You may feel that when this person died, part of you died with him or her. And now you are faced with finding some meaning in going on with your life even though you may at times feel empty.

This death calls for you to confront your own spirituality as well as your overall philosophy of life. You may have spiritual conflicts and questions racing through your head and heart. This is normal and part of your journey toward renewed living.

You might feel distant from your God or Higher Power, even questioning their very existence. You may rage at your God. Again, such feelings of doubt are normal. Remember—mourners often find themselves questioning their faith for months, sometimes years, before they rediscover meaning in life. But be assured: It can be done, even when you don't have all the answers.

Early in grief, allow yourself to openly mourn without pressuring yourself to have answers to profound meaning of life questions. Move at your own pace as you recognize that allowing yourself to hurt and find continued meaning to live are not mutually exclusive. More often, your need to mourn and your need to find meaning in your continued living will blend into each other, with the former very slowly giving way to the latter as healing occurs.

In my experience, the grief that comes with suicide demands that you dose the pain as you do this search for meaning work. In other words, befriending your pain is only a part of the healing. Without nourishing our need to search for meaning that invites you to go on

TURNING TO CEREMONY TO FACILITATE MOURNING

As you work on the six needs of mourning over time, actively embracing and expressing your grief, you can also add in the power of ceremony to encourage your active mourning. Long after the funeral, ceremonies that combine intentionality, actions, symbolism, sequence, presence, heart, and spirit can also give your grief divine momentum.

Group memory ceremonies (sometimes hosted by hospices or funeral homes); family cemetery visits, tree plantings, or memorial runs in honor of a loved one; annual fundraisers to support a nonprofit or cause dear to the person who died; and gatherings that mark the anniversary of the death are a few common examples. Such ceremonies help grievers meet their ongoing needs of mourning. You can pick and choose the forms of ceremony that feel right for you. But you can also carry out personal grief ceremonies by yourself at any time in the privacy of your own home. For more guidance and ceremony ideas, you might want to see my book *Grief Day by Day: Simple Practices to Help Yourself Survive...and Thrive.*

I hope you'll try some ongoing ceremonies. If you do, I believe you'll marvel at their power. Death transforms love into grief, and ceremony helps transform grief into healing.

living, the pain can eat away at you, leaving you feeling naked in the world. I have seen this happen when there is what I call a lack of nourishment surrounding the search for meaning. So, I say search away, and as you do, remember someone very wise once reminded me that "the heart of faith is believing one is never alone." Please don't allow yourself to feel alone in your search. Find compassionate companions who will accompany you on this wilderness journey.

EXPRESS YOURSELF:
Go to *The Understanding Your Suicide Grief Journal* on pp. 119-121.

MOURNING NEED 6:

Let Others Help You—Now and Always

The quality and quantity of understanding support you get during your work of mourning will have a major influence on your capacity to integrate this loss into your life. You cannot—nor should you try to—do this alone. Drawing on the experiences and encouragement of friends, fellow mourners, and/or professional counselors is not a weakness but a healthy human need. And because mourning is a process that takes place over time, this support must be available months and even years after the suicide death of someone in your life.

Unfortunately, because our society places so much value on the ability to "carry on," "keep your chin up," and "keep busy," many people experiencing grief are abandoned shortly after the event of the death. "It's best not to talk about death," "It's over and done with," and "It's time to get on with your life" are the types of messages directed at grieving people that sometimes still dominate, particularly when suicide is the cause of the death. Obviously, these messages encourage you to deny or repress your grief rather than express it.

If you know people who consider themselves supportive yet offer you these kinds of mourning-avoidant attitudes, you'll need to look

A SURVIVOR SPEAKS

"Faith has always been a big part of my life. This suicide death brought me some "whys?" that left me having words with God. The good news is that I found out he could take my questions, and I was able to search. The search led me to find renewal, and while I'll always miss John, my best testimony is to live as well as I can from a place of purpose... and that is just what I have been able to do."

to others for truly helpful support. People who see your mourning as something that should be overcome instead of experienced will not help you come out of the dark and into the light.

To be truly helpful, the people in your support system must appreciate the impact this death has had on you. They must understand that in order to heal, you must be allowed—even encouraged—to mourn long after the death. And they must encourage you to see mourning not as an enemy to be vanquished but rather as a necessity to be experienced as a result of having loved. Perhaps you are surrounded by just such people. If you are receiving excellent support from friends and family, you're fortunate. I encourage you to have gratitude and grace.

You will also probably discover, if you haven't already, that you can benefit from a connectedness that comes from people who have also had a suicide death in their lives. The credo of The Compassionate Friends, an international organization of grieving parents, is "You need not walk alone." I might add, "You cannot walk alone." **Support groups, where people come together and share the common bond of experience, can be invaluable in helping you and supporting your need to mourn long after the death.**

You will learn more about support groups and how to create support systems for yourself later in this book. But, for right now, remind yourself that you deserve and need to have understanding

A SURVIVOR SPEAKS

"I cannot express how helpful it has been to make use of certain friends who have been understanding and supportive. My true friends and my support group have held my hand and walked with me from the start... and, to show their true wisdom, they realize there is no set finish line I am supposed to reach."

people around you who allow you to feel and share your grief long after our culture tends to deem appropriate.

EXPRESS YOURSELF:
Go to *The Understanding Your Suicide Grief Journal* on pp. 122-123.

Journeying with the Six Needs

I have been honored to be a grief companion to thousands of suicide loss survivors. Without exception, I've found that mourners are helped by the concept of the six central needs of mourning. There is a lot of information in this book, but if you were to commit to memory one small part, I would recommend that it be these six needs of mourning. Upholding and fulfilling these six needs over time will help you understand how you have been forever changed by this loss. I would also encourage you to revisit this chapter now and then in the future and review your progress in meeting these needs.

The consequences of not attending to the six needs of mourning, on the other hand, can be devastating. If you don't actively engage with and express the six needs of mourning on an ongoing basis, you may remain stuck or lost in the wilderness of your grief. I'll talk more about this in Touchstone Eight, but for now, I hope you'll remember that these six needs are your guide and your friend.

Recognize You Are Not Crazy

In all my years as a grief counselor, the most common question mourners have asked me is, "Am I going crazy?" The second most common question is, "Am I normal?" The journey through grief can be so radically different from our everyday realities that sometimes it feels more like being picked up and dropped onto the surface of the moon than it does a trek through the wilderness. The terrain is so very foreign and disorienting, and our behaviors in that terrain seem so out of the ordinary, that we feel like we're going crazy.

> "I had melancholy thoughts... A strangeness in my mind. A feeling that I was not for that hour, nor for that place."
>
> William Wordsworth

Experiencing something that may seem "crazy" can be a very natural response when coping with the death of someone in your life, and particularly with the special features of a suicide loss. Because the grief that accompanies a death to suicide can be painful and overwhelming, it can be very scary and leave you questioning your sanity. Many survivors have taught me that they wonder if they are mourning in the "right way" and question if the feelings and experiences they have are normal.

For example, I once counseled a woman whose husband had died by suicide. She came in for counseling and would follow the instinct to keep retelling the story of his suicide death. After several meetings she began to think there was something wrong with her because she felt the need to, in her words, "compulsively go over what happened again and again." As compassionately as I could, I helped her come to understand that she was doing exactly what she needed to do. With time and retelling, she became less of a numb witness and began to gently embrace the reality of her husband's death to suicide. Now, years later, she has gone on to help many other survivors understand the need to "retell the story" and realize they

WHAT I MEAN BY CRAZY

The term "crazy" is no longer considered acceptable in mental-health circles. Rightfully so. It stigmatizes mental-health issues and places blame and shame on those who suffer from mental-health challenges.

However, "crazy" is in fact the term I've heard grieving people use most often to describe their own early-grief experiences of shock, disorientation, protest emotions, and more. Actually, they almost always use the word "crazy" to collectively label all their early-grief symptoms.

The word "crazy" comes to us from the 14th century Germanic word *crasen*, which meant "to shatter, crush, break into pieces." Before that existed the Old Norse *krasa*, which also meant "to shatter."

If you pick up an old piece of fine china, you might see a web of fine lines on its surface. This is called "crazing." The glaze, normally transparent and invisible, has shattered into tiny sections.

Early grief, particularly after a suicide, is equally shattering. It crushes us and breaks us into a million pieces. This experience tends to make us feel, well, crazed for a while – for weeks, months, and sometimes even years.

So I decided to use the term "crazy" in this touchstone title after all. I agree it's not an appropriate term for mental illnesses because it carries too much baggage and stigma. But grief, which is not an illness, often feels crazy in the truest sense of the word because it can shatter you, crush you, and make you feel like you've broken into pieces.

are not "crazy." She now realizes that the retelling of the story of the suicide death is often fundamental to anyone connected to the person who is now gone.

The woman wasn't crazy, and you're not either. You may be experiencing thoughts and feelings that seem crazy because they are so unusual to you, but what is unusual in life is often usual in grief.

This touchstone helps you be on the lookout for the trail marker that affirms your sanity. It's an important trail marker, because if you miss it, your entire journey through the wilderness of your grief may feel like Alice's surreal visit to Wonderland. Actually, your journey may still feel surreal even if you find this trail marker, but at least you'll know in your head that you're not going crazy.

Following are a number of common thoughts and feelings in grief that cause mourners to feel like they're going crazy. They may or may not be part of your personal experience. As I've said, my intent is not to prescribe what should be happening to you. Instead, I encourage you to become familiar with what you may encounter while you grieve and do your hard work of mourning.

Sudden Changes in Mood

The grief that comes with this journey can make you feel like you are surviving fairly well one minute and in the depths of despair the next. Sudden changes in your mood are a difficult, yet natural, part of your experience. You are on an "emotional and spiritual roller-coaster." These mood changes can be small or dramatic. They can be set off by driving past a familiar place, the lyrics of a song, an insensitive comment made by someone, a change in the seasons, a change in the weather, or simply waking up in the morning to a new day without this person in your life.

Mood changes can make you feel like you are going crazy because you may have been told "Time heals all wounds" and believe you should follow a pattern of continued motion forward. In other words, you may expect yourself to keep feeling better and better each and every day. In reality, your emotions twist and turn and go up and down like a mountainous trail. One minute you might be feeling okay, or at least surviving, and the next, deeply depressed and inconsolable.

A SURVIVOR SPEAKS

"I was okay one moment and then sobbing the next. To say it is like riding a rollercoaster is an understatement. I felt like it was a tsunami!"

If you have these sudden changes in mood, don't be hard on yourself. In my experience, more survivors have these mood swings than those who don't. It may be little consolation to know you may be in the majority, but I don't want you thinking something is wrong with you. Be patient with yourself. As you actively mourn and receive the support you deserve, the periods of despair and darkness will be interspersed with more periods of lightness and hope.

EXPRESS YOURSELF:
Go to *The Understanding Your Suicide Grief Journal* on p. 126.

Memory Lapses and Time Distortion

Short-term memory can disappear as you encounter this experience. Entire blocks of time may be blocked from your memory. Long-term memory may still be with you, but short-term memory—such as what you did yesterday or where you just put something—often diminishes.

Time may also feel very distorted, meaning that sometimes, time moves quickly; at other times, it crawls. Your sense of past and future may seem to be frozen in place. You may lose track of what day, month, or even year it is. Your memory lapses and your inability to keep time right now aren't crazy. They are very common in suicide grief. Remember—you have been torn apart and have unique needs. Find practical ways to help yourself, such as writing down what you are going to buy when you go to the store. Otherwise, if you are in any way like I was, or many people I have counseled, you may forget what you went to get!

EXPRESS YOURSELF:
Go to *The Understanding Your Suicide Grief Journal* on p. 126.

Polyphasic Behavior and Thinking Challenges

This is a fancy-sounding term that means you start doing something and then, right in the middle of it, you forget what you are doing and start doing something else. Many a survivor has shared with me experiences like having started to wash the dishes, then remembering they forgot to finish making the bed, then remembering it was garbage day and they had forgotten to take the garbage out.

These kind of scattered behaviors, where it is difficult to stay "on task," often go hand-in-hand with an inability to stay focused. This is often referred to as "brain fog." You may experience the loss of your train of thought for what seems like hours at a time. Again, you will need to be self-compassionate and patient before you see these experiences soften ever so slowly over time.

A SURVIVOR SPEAKS

"I would have to write a check, but I could not recall the date to save myself. I had to try to remember, although I often forgot, to carry a little calendar in my pocket."

A SURVIVOR SPEAKS

"Actually, I felt like I had some form of dementia. I would start to try to accomplish something and then, right in the middle of what I was doing, I would go blank and just start doing something else."

EXPRESS YOURSELF:
Go to *The Understanding Your Suicide Grief Journal* on p. 127.

Psychic Numbing, Dissociation, Disconnection

As noted in Touchstone Four (and it is so important I review it again here), "psychic numbing" is like a bandage that your psyche has placed over your wound. The bandage protects the wound until it becomes less raw and open. You may feel like you are present but not accounted for. This has been described to me as "watching myself from the outside in." Remember, temporarily this psychic numbing is a great gift that actually helps you survive. Your emotions are being given the needed time to catch up to what your mind has been told.

Dissociation is a close cousin of psychic numbing. It is where your emotions are split off from your thoughts because they are too overwhelming to encounter. You may feel detached from your feelings, like you are in slow-motion. You may find yourself questioning why the full reality of what happened seems so "unreal" to you. Again, this is survival-oriented and not only natural but actually helpful to you.

The phenomenon of disconnection is hard to put into words. However, allow me to try. When someone dies from natural causes such as old age, or even in an accident, I have learned it is sometimes easier than with a death from a suicide to retain happy memories. You recognize that if they could, the person who died would still want to be here with you. With suicide, on the other hand, your connection to happy memories may be more complicated. Because the person seems to have made a choice that is so painful to you, you may be more at risk for being disconnected from pleasant, even very happy memories of them. This makes doing the memory work I describe in Touchstone 5 (see p. 139) even more important.

Let me assure you that you can and will be able to restore happy memories of the person who died, but I ask you to go slow and reach out to compassionate people who will support you. Yes, precious memories of good times will return to you because "death ends a life, not a relationship." This potential barrier to recalling happy memories appears to be a natural phenomenon related to the circumstances of the death. Yet, again, allow me to gently remind you, your memories can and will come back and embrace you with love and grace.

EXPRESS YOURSELF:
Go to *The Understanding Your Suicide Grief Journal* on p. 127.

Self-Focus or Feeling Selfish

Especially early in your grief, you may find yourself being less conscious of the needs of others. You may not want to listen to other people's life challenges or problems, feeling like they pale in comparison to what you are faced with. You may not have the energy to attend to the needs of your children or other family members. You may feel angry or disheartened that the world is still turning while your life feels frozen in time.

A SURVIVOR SPEAKS

"At first, and for longer than I would have liked, I could not remember any of the times of joy and happiness with Larry. But, slowly those times have come back to me, and I'm so very thankful. Sometimes I feel what I learned to refer to as sappy—sad yet happy all at once. And sometimes now I'm totally happy as I recall his smile and how he made me laugh, even when I didn't feel like it."

The reality is that during this experience, you are less tuned into the needs of others and are instead focusing on your own thoughts and feelings. However, this doesn't mean you are crazy or selfish. What it does mean is that you have emotional and spiritual needs that are demanding you give more attention and energy to yourself right now. Your mind and your spirit are directing your attention away from others and onto yourself because you need to do this to integrate your grief into your life. Please do not shame yourself if you feel like this fits with your experiences. Feeling like you are "turned inward" is a necessary part of your grief work. I refer to this as the "cocooning phenomenon." You mourn from the inside to the outside, so this phenomenon is not only natural, it is necessary!

Later on you will be ready to reconnect with others and provide support to them. The capacity to eventually give outside of yourself requires that you first and foremost receive right now.

If you need help caring for dependent children or elderly parents, try to find some caring friends and family who can assist you for a while. Of course, the needs of other people you care about (like children, spouses, significant others, parents, friends, and pets) are very important. However, it is okay to acknowledge that these are times when you are unable to be as available to them as you'd like and need to call in reinforcements.

Some people may attempt to take your grief away from you by trying to keep you from any self-focus. They may want you to quickly reenter the "regular" world because they don't understand your need for a temporary retreat. If turning inward is part of your experience, be assured you are normal.

When you are in pain after a death to suicide, turning inward and the need for self-focus is analogous to what occurs when you have a physical wound. You cover a physical wound with a bandage for a period of time. Then you expose the wound to the open air, which helps with healing but also risks contamination. The emotional, physical, and spiritual pain that accompanies a suicide death demands the same kind of protection.

However, the word temporary is important here. You may move back and forth between needing time alone and needing time with other people. If you stay in a self-focused, inward mode, you may risk developing a pattern of not expressing how your grief is impacting you. As you well know by now, not expressing yourself and exploring how your life is reshaped by this experience will influence your ability to integrate this loss into your life.

EXPRESS YOURSELF:
Go to *The Understanding Your Suicide Grief Journal* on p. 128.

Rethinking and Restorative Retelling of the Story

While I introduced this important phenomenon in Touchstone Four, it is so vital that I believe we should *retell* a little bit about it again here. As you learned in the fourth touchstone, "Restorative Retelling" isn't a sign that you're going crazy; in fact, it's a sign that you're doing the work of mourning.

Whether you are conscious of it or not, you retell yourself the story and retell others the story in an effort to ultimately help yourself integrate the death into your life. What you have experienced—the death of someone to suicide—is so difficult to fathom that your mind compels you to revisit it again and again until you have truly acknowledged and embraced its reality. Telling the story slowly helps bring your head and heart together.

Allow yourself this necessary review. Don't be upset with yourself if you cannot seem to stop repeating your story, whether in your mind or aloud to others. The retelling of your story is an inherent need as you wander through the wilderness. Most people have taught me that it is the retelling that in essence helps your journey soften over time. This may seem counter-intuitive, yet I invite you to have the courage to trust this unfolding, deeply spiritual process.

Do watch out for people (both professional caregivers and laypeople), who have not been sensitized or grief-informed to the valuable function of retelling your story. These people may say hurtful things such as, "Obsessing over what happened won't change anything" or "You need to put the past in the past and get on with your life." Or, worse yet, "You need to let go and have closure." Remember—these are misinformed people who have often created defenses that do not allow them to tolerate the pain of your traumatic loss. Blocking your need to retell the story will not help you on your path to integrating this death into your life.

A SURVIVOR SPEAKS

"For a while I seemed possessed by the need to revisit and retell what happened. As I now look back, I realize this urgent need to revisit what happened was essential to forming a story. I didn't understand it at the time. I just did it... and fortunately after a few missteps I found the safe people who allowed and encouraged me to do it. For that I say... thank God!"

Yes, it often hurts to revisit the suicide death. But remember—grief wounds require going backward before you can go forward. Be compassionate with yourself. Surround yourself with people who allow and encourage you to repeat whatever you need to repeat. Support groups are helpful to many people because there is a wisdom and mutual understanding of the need to "retell the story." I strongly believe that when you allow yourself to restory your life, grace happens!

EXPRESS YOURSELF:
Go to *The Understanding Your Suicide Grief Journal* on p. 128.

Powerlessness and Helplessness
The trauma of suicide grief can at times leave you feeling powerless.

You may think or say, "What am I going to do? I feel so completely helpless." While part of you realizes you had no control over what happened, another part might feel a sense of powerlessness at not having been able to prevent it. You would like to have your life back the way it was, but you can't. You may think, hope, wish, and pray the death could be reversed, but feel powerless in the knowledge that it can't be.

Also, you may wonder that if somehow you or someone else would have acted differently or been more assertive, you could have prevented the death. Your "if onlys" and "what ifs" are often expressions of wishing you could have been more powerful or in control of something you could not. Lack of control is a difficult reality to accept, yet it is one that, over time and through the work of mourning, you must encounter. These feelings of helplessness and powerlessness in the face of this painful reality are normal and natural.

Almost paradoxically, by acknowledging and allowing for temporary feelings of helplessness, you help yourself. When you try to "stay strong," you often get yourself into trouble. Share your feelings with caring people around you. Remember—shared grief is diminished grief; find someone to talk to who will listen without judging.

EXPRESS YOURSELF:
Go to *The Understanding Your Suicide Grief Journal* on p. 128.

Loss of Energy and the Lethargy of Grief
Experiencing trauma grief is physically demanding. Your body responds to the overwhelming stress and lets you know it has

unique needs. You may well lack energy and feel highly fatigued and weak. You are probably not sleeping very well and your appetite may be affected with either lack of desire to eat or the tendency to overeat.

You may be more susceptible to illness and physical discomforts. I will explore this more with you in Touchstone Seven, but for now, do know that your body has these unique needs and will keep asking you to take good care of it. For more help in caring for your body you might refer to my book titled *Healing Your Grieving Body: 100 Physical Practices for Mourners.*

EXPRESS YOURSELF:
Go to *The Understanding Your Suicide Grief Journal* on p. 129.

A Feeling of Before the Suicide and After the Suicide

When someone in your life dies by suicide, there is often a Before and an After. There is your life Before the suicide, and now there is your life After the suicide. It's as if your internal calendar gets reset to mark the significance of the profound loss.

Some, certainly not all, people I have counseled at my Center for Loss have told me, without much thought or conscious calculation, they know how many years, months, and days it has been since the suicide death. This new way of keeping time is perfectly natural. You are not crazy! Your mind and heart have simply come up with a new system to mark the earth's relentless motion.

I have also found that it is normal for your newfound timekeeping system to come up in some of your interactions with people around you. When, and if, it does for you, realize some people will project they are uncomfortable that you do this. You will discover quickly who understands this "resetting of your clock" and who doesn't.

EXPRESS YOURSELF:
Go to *The Understanding Your Suicide Grief Journal* on p. 129.

A SURVIVOR SPEAKS

"Yes, it is like there was a before and an after. Sometimes I can sense that people wish I didn't think of life that way, but I do and I cannot change that reality."

A SURVIVOR SPEAKS

"I didn't use to say those words I love you much at all. But now I can't keep from saying them to the people who mean so very much to me."

Expressing Feelings More Openly Than in the Past

This suicide death sometimes makes you more aware of how love makes the world go round. Now, you may find yourself not sitting on feelings you do have and being more expressive to people you care deeply about.

Sometimes we love people so much, we forget to tell them "I love you." Or, we (mistakenly) believe that they know they are loved, so we don't need to tell them. After a death to suicide, this changes for many of us.

You may now discover that these three simple yet profound words have deep, spiritual meaning to you. Where in the past you may have hesitated to say these words, they may now come easily from your lips. You may even find that some people don't understand your need to remind them they are loved! But that is okay; you just keep on telling them!

EXPRESS YOURSELF:
Go to *The Understanding Your Suicide Grief Journal* on p. 129.

Griefbursts

"I was doing pretty well, when out of nowhere came this overwhelming wave of grief!" Has this happened to you?

I call this experience a "griefburst"—a sudden, sharp feeling of grief that causes anxiety and pain. Some people call them grief attacks because they often attack without warning.

Before they come to grief, many people expect grief to be made up mostly of long periods of deep depression. Actually, after the early weeks, what you're more likely to encounter are acute and episodic pangs or spasms of grief in between relatively pain-free hours.

Examples of griefbursts might include visiting places you traveled together, either coming across or seeing people who loved the person who died, or experiencing activities he or she loved to do. For example, you are at the beach and are suddenly struck by remembering how much he or she loved being by the water.

During a griefburst, you may feel an overwhelming sense of missing the person you love and find yourself openly crying or sobbing. As one widow told me, "I'll be busy for a while, and sometimes even forget he has died. Then I'll see his picture or smell his favorite food, and I'll just feel like I can't even move."

Griefbursts may feel like "crazybursts," but they're normal. When and if one strikes you, be compassionate with yourself. You have every right to experience intense pangs of missing the person who died and to feel temporary paralysis or loss of control. Whatever you do, don't try to deny or suppress griefbursts when they come over you. It's powerful because it wants and needs your attention. I also like to think of griefbursts as evidence that those we love are determined not to be forgotten.

Although the pain of a griefburst hurts so deeply, allow it to wash over you. If you'd feel more comfortable, retreat to a private place where you can wail or scream or do whatever you need to do. After

A SURVIVOR SPEAKS

"I would be rolling along through my day and then I'd see someone who would drive past in a car just like hers. That is all it would take, and I'd start crying like there was no tomorrow."

A SURVIVOR SPEAKS

"As I look back, I remember just crying like I would never run out of tears. But I always felt better after a good cry. So, I say let the tears flow. You may think they will never stop, but they will... and then they will come again when they need to."

it passes, talk about your griefburst with someone who cares about you.

EXPRESS YOURSELF:
Go to *The Understanding Your Suicide Grief Journal* on p. 130.

Crying and Sobbing

If you're crying and sobbing a lot, you may feel like you never will stop, which can trigger your feelings of going crazy. Sobbing is like wailing, and it comes from the inner core of your being. Sobbing is an expression of the deep, strong emotions within you. These emotions need to get out, and sobbing allows for their release.

In many Eastern cultures, sobbing and wailing (sometimes called *keening*) are encouraged and understood as a normal part of grief and mourning life's losses. However, in Western culture, sobbing is often considered strange and feels frightening to observers. It is perceived as being "out of control" or "dramatic." The reality is you do not have control of this situation, and it is this very loss of control that helps you express your strong feelings. Your feelings are too strong to be "under control" inside you—and their authentic expression can't be under control either.

If you're crying or sobbing a lot, you're not crazy. Cry, wail, and sob as long and as hard and as often as you need to. Don't try to be strong and brave for yourself or anyone else. Tears have a voice of their own. You will be wise to allow yours to speak to you.

EXPRESS YOURSELF:
Go to *The Understanding Your Suicide Grief Journal* on p. 130.

BORROWED TEARS

Here's another kind of crying that can make you feel like you're going crazy: borrowed tears. Borrowed tears are those that spring up when you're suddenly and often unexpectedly touched by something you might see, hear, or smell, and you react with strong emotion. During a griefburst, you might be brought to tears by a place or a smell that reminds you of the person who died. Borrowed tears, on the other hand, seem to come out of nowhere and are triggered by something you don't associate with the person who died and wouldn't normally be upset by.

Borrowed tears are called this because you seem to be borrowing them from someone else's store of pain and memory. They're not yours! For example, you might find yourself crying at a sappy TV commercial or seeing a little bird out your window. These things never made you sad before. Why are you crying now?

A SURVIVOR SPEAKS

"I was watching a simple movie with a friend, and something one of the characters said about love just touched me in a special place and I started weeping. I guess I needed a good cry. Well, I sure got one!"

You're crying because your heart and soul are hurting and your emotions are tender. Think of it this way: If you press on your leg gently with your hand, it doesn't hurt. But if you break your leg and then press on it, even the slightest touch can hurt. Your heart is broken now, and anything that touches your heart even slightly (including happy or beautiful things) may hurt a lot. This is normal and will soften as you allow yourself to mourn.

Linking Objects and Memorabilia

Linking objects are items that belonged to the person who died that you now like to have around you. Objects such as clothing, books, knick-knacks, furniture, artwork, and other prized possessions can help you feel physically close to the person you miss so much.

Once when I was counseling a widow, she shared with me that she found it comforting to take one of her husband's shirts to bed with her. She said that as she clutched his shirt close to her, she didn't feel so alone. But as she allowed herself to mourn, her need to have the shirt close to her eventually softened.

If you like to hold, be near, look at, sleep with, caress, even smell a special belonging of the person who is dead, you're not crazy. You're simply trying to hold on to a tangible, physical connection to the person. The person's body is no longer physically here, but these special items are. Like the woman who slept with her husband's shirt, you will probably need your linking objects less and less over time, as you integrate the loss into your life. But you may always find these items special and want to keep them.

I suggest you also not rush into giving away the belongings of the person who died. Sometimes people hurry into clearing out all the "stuff" because they think it will help them feel better. It usually doesn't. In fact, getting rid of the belongings because they're too painful to have around is antithetical to the touchstones described in this book. Opening to the presence of the loss may include embracing the feelings that are stirred up by the belongings of the person who died by suicide. If you get rid of the belongings prematurely, you may later find yourself wishing that you had some of them back. So a simple reminder to go slow.

I'd also like to point out the difference between cherishing some belongings and creating a "shrine." Mourners create a shrine when for years (sometimes decades) after the death they keep everything just as it was when the person died. Unlike keeping linking objects, creating a long-term shrine often prevents you from acknowledging the painful new reality that someone you love has died. It's as if unconsciously you expect the person to return to you at any moment.

When the death is from suicide, I often find that you need to keep belongings close to you longer than many people around you may be comfortable with. Watch out for these people, and don't let them rush you out of their needs instead of yours. You will always want to keep some special objects and memorabilia that connect you to this person. If you are concerned about your attachment to belongings that connect you to the person who died, consider exploring this with a compassionate grief-informed counselor. There is nothing wrong with having photos up in your home and displaying some items that reflect your reality that love doesn't end when a death occurs. Go at your own pace and remember—once you have given something away or disposed of it, you often cannot get it back.

A SURVIVOR SPEAKS

"I have some pictures of my son up in the house and to me that only seems right. I did have one friend ask me if it was a shrine. So, I said, no it is a temple and just laughed. I know some people think you should get rid of reminders, but I couldn't disagree more. It doesn't mean I'm denying he is dead; it just helps me feel closer to him than I would otherwise."

EXPRESS YOURSELF:
Go to *The Understanding Your Suicide Grief Journal* on p. 130.

Suicidal Thoughts

We touched on suicidal thoughts in Touchstone Four, but this subject is important enough to reemphasize here. Thoughts that come and go about questioning if you want to go on living can be a normal part of your grief and mourning. You might say or think,

"It'd be so much easier not to be here" or "I'm not sure I'd mind if I didn't wake up tomorrow." Usually these thoughts are not so much an active wish to die as they are a wish to avoid or ease your pain.

To have these thoughts is normal and not crazy; however, to make plans and take action to end your life is extremely concerning and not a normal response to this tragic death. Sometimes your body, mind, and spirit can hurt so much that you wonder if you will ever feel alive again. Just remember that in doing the hard work of mourning, you can and will find continued meaning in life. Let yourself be helped as you discover hope for your healing.

If thoughts of suicide take on planning and structure, make certain that you get help immediately. Sometimes tunnel vision can prevent you from seeing choices. You have the capacity to mourn this death and go on to rediscover a life filled with meaning and purpose. Also keep a close watch on other friends and family members grieving this death. If you notice any signs that might indicate suicidal plans, get professional help immediately.

A SURVIVOR SPEAKS

"Early on I thought I should just join her and take my own life. But then I thought that wouldn't be of any help to anyone, including myself. I found a terrific counselor who helped me through this. If you have any thoughts like this, get help as soon as possible. I did and it made a huge difference for me."

EXPRESS YOURSELF:
Go to *The Understanding Your Suicide Grief Journal* on p. 131.

Drugs or Alcohol Use

When someone dies, you may be tempted to quickly quell your feelings of grief. This desire to avoid and mask the pain is understandable. The trouble is, using drugs and alcohol to help you do so only brings temporary relief from a hurt that must ultimately be embraced.

For example, a well-meaning friend hands you a bottle of sleeping pills and says, "Take one tonight. You need your sleep." Or you find yourself sipping wine to get through each evening. Should you take these substances?

First, never take prescription drugs unless they were prescribed for you by a medical provider. You don't know how you might react to a certain medication, and they should be monitored carefully in collaboration with a qualified provider.

Don't take a medication that your doctor has prescribed, either, unless you understand and agree with the reasons for taking it and the effects it may have on you. If you need more information, ask. Drugs that make you feel numb or unnaturally peaceful may only complicate your grief experience. After all, they will eventually wear off, and you will still have to struggle with the pain. Psychological or physical dependence can also be a problem with some medications. If your doctor has prescribed a drug to help you cope with your grief, you may want to get a second opinion.

Alcohol is yet another danger for grieving people. When you drink, you may indeed feel better—temporarily. But alcohol taken to mask painful feelings is only a crutch and when overused, may in fact cause an entirely new set of problems. The same goes for marijuana and other controlled substances.

This is not to say that grieving people should never take medications. For example, you may become so sleep-deprived that temporary use of a sedative, anti-anxiety medication, or sleep aid is warranted. And of course, if clinical depression arises (as previously noted on page 124), taking prescribed antidepressants may well be an essential, lifesaving part of your care plan. It is also important to note that people who were taking antidepressants prior to the death of someone loved should continue taking them afterward as prescribed by a provider. When appropriately prescribed, your grief will not be further complicated by the use of these medications.

EXPRESS YOURSELF:
Go to *The Understanding Your Suicide Grief Journal* on p. 131.

A SURVIVOR SPEAKS

"In hindsight I realized I started self-treating my grief to try to relieve my pain. It only seemed to work temporarily and finally I realized it was actually self-destructive."

Dreams or Nightmares

Sometimes dreaming a lot about the person who died may contribute to your feelings of going crazy. Mourners sometimes tell me that they can't stop thinking about the death—even in their sleep!

Keep in mind that dreams are one of the ways the work of mourning takes place. For example, a dream may reflect a searching and yearning for the person who has died. You may dream that you are with the person in a crowded place and lose him and cannot find him. Dreams also provide opportunities—to feel close to the person who died, to embrace the reality of the death, to gently confront the depth of the loss, to renew memories, or to develop a new self-identity. Dreams also may help you search for meaning in life and death or explore unfinished business. Finally, dreams can often provide you hope for the future.

The content of your dreams often reflects changes in your grief journey. You may have one kind of dream early in your grief and another later on. So if dreams are part of your trek through the wilderness, make use of them to better understand where you have been, where you are, and where you are going. Also, find a skilled listener who won't interpret your dreams for you, but who will listen to you.

It is one thing to dream, it is another to experience nightmares that frighten and disturb you. Nightmares sometimes reflect the need for what is called "trauma processing." If nightmares are part of your experience, I urge you to see a professional caregiver who can help you sort out what is going on.

Remember—a good counselor can be a companion, a guide into and through your journey. Don't suffer through nightmares alone or in isolation—get help now!

A SURVIVOR SPEAKS

"I found that my nightmares reflected the trauma I had experienced. Some members of my support groups had comforting dreams, but I had nightmares that intruded into my entire being. I got help sorting out what was going on, and that helped me in so many ways. Eventually my nightmares stopped and a few comforting dreams came along. I liked the dreams, I couldn't tolerate the nightmares!"

EXPRESS YOURSELF:
Go to *The Understanding Your Suicide Grief Journal* on pp. 131-132.

Mystical Experiences

When someone you love dies, you may have experiences that are not always rationally explainable. That doesn't mean you're crazy!

If you share these experiences with others, they may question your mental fitness, however. But I like to say that if you have mystical experiences, you're simply mystically sensitive.

The primary form of mystical experience that grieving people have taught me about is communicating with the person who died. This ranges from sensing a presence or feeling a touch to hearing a voice, seeing a vision, receiving a sign, and many more.

What constitutes a mystical experience in grief can vary greatly. In Alabama, for example, a mother whose daughter had died woke up one summer morning only to find it snowing in her backyard (and her backyard only)! The snow lasted for fifteen minutes and then stopped. The mother understood this as a communication telling her that her daughter was all right and that she shouldn't worry so much. In another instance, a man whose wife had died saw her lying on the couch in their living room. "It's like she came to me and wrapped me in her arms. I felt warm and happy...I experienced her presence," he said.

A SURVIVOR SPEAKS

"I was sitting in my living room when I had this very strong sense of his presence. It was like he was right there, wanting to wrap his arms around me but didn't know if it would scare me. So, I said aloud, go ahead and hug me... and he did... then he slipped away. It was like he was just letting me know he was okay. I have learned I have to watch who I tell about this."

Some people find these experiences hard to believe and explain them away in a rational manner: "I must have been dreaming" or "I was probably half-asleep." Others try to distance themselves from these experiences because they have been taught that such things are impossible: "A rational mind just doesn't experience those kinds of things." So, if you want to be considered rational or sane (and who doesn't!), you might feel compelled to distance yourself from these kinds of experiences.

But I have listened to and learned from hundreds of people who believe they have received some form of communication from those who have died. If you count yourself among them, you're not going crazy. You can still be very sane and exceedingly rational while at times experiencing and embracing mystical encounters. Who on this earth is to say what's real and what isn't? Certainly not I. Remain open to these experiences and be thankful for any comfort they provide.

EXPRESS YOURSELF:
Go to *The Understanding Your Suicide Grief Journal* on p. 132.

Anniversaries, Holidays, and Special Occasions

Naturally, anniversaries, holidays, and special occasions can bring about pangs of grief. Birthdays, wedding dates, holidays such as Easter, Thanksgiving, Hanukkah, and Christmas, and other special occasions often create a heightened sense of loss. At these times, you may likely experience griefbursts.

Your pangs of grief also may occur in circumstances that bring up reminders of the painful absence of someone in your life. For many families, certain days have special meaning (for example, the first snowfall, an annual Fourth of July party, or any time when activities were shared as a couple or a family), and the person who died is more deeply missed at those times.

Of course, on these special occasions you may not only miss the person who died, you may also be mourning the loss of hopes and dreams for the future. If your unmarried child died by suicide, for example, special occasions such as weddings or christenings will likely stir up regrets that you and your family will never experience the joy of these occasions in the life of your child.

If you're having a really tough time on special days, you're not crazy. Perhaps the most important thing to remember is that your feelings are natural. And sometimes the anticipation of an anniversary or holiday turns out to be worse than the day itself.

Interestingly, sometimes your internal clock will alert you to an anniversary date you may not consciously be aware of. If you notice you are feeling down or experiencing pangs of grief, you may be having an anniversary response. Take a look at the calendar and consider if this particular day or time of the year has meant anything to you in years past.

Plan ahead when you know some naturally painful times are coming. Unfortunately, some grieving people will not mention anniversaries, holidays, or special occasions to anyone. So they suffer in silence, and their feelings of isolation increase. Don't let this happen to you. Recognize you will need support, and map out how to get it!

"Thanksgiving was always Dad's favorite gathering time. Now, every year as it approaches, I have learned to take very special care of myself. I survive it, but I think it will always be greeted with some sadness."

EXPRESS YOURSELF:
Go to *The Understanding Your Suicide Grief Journal* on p. 133.

Ritual-Stimulated Reactions, Seasonal Reactions, Music-Stimulated Reactions, and Age-Correspondence Reactions

Similar to griefbursts in nature, certain experiences you encounter might re-stimulate feelings surrounding your loss. Four such forms are briefly outlined below.

RITUAL-STIMULATED REACTIONS are things like gathering for family dinners or a Sunday brunch. You may have been used to this being a special time with your precious person and naturally feel his or her absence.

SEASONAL REACTIONS relate to how the change of seasons can stimulate grief or invite you to slow down and continue to honor your ongoing need to mourn. Be gentle with yourself as the seasons change and nurture yourself if you know you are more prone to being depressed at a particular time of year.

MUSIC-STIMULATED GRIEF relates to how music can activate your right brain, creating associations and deep, often profound feelings stimulated by a specific song or piece of music.

AGE-CORRESPONDENCE REACTIONS can take place, for example, when you reach a certain age at which someone was when they died by suicide. So, if your parent died at age 62, when you reach that age you may naturally experience a renewed sense of loss.

EXPRESS YOURSELF:
Go to *The Understanding Your Suicide Grief Journal* on p. 133.

The Crazy Things People Say and Do

Sometimes in grief, other people may make you feel crazy. What you really need at this time is acceptance, affirmation, and nonjudgment. However, some people may imply or tell you that your natural grief response is abnormal or wrong.

Platitudes are one way this can happen. You may have heard some of these gems:

"At least you had him as long as you did."

"You just need to put the past in the past."

"Just keep your chin up!"

"You need to keep busy and not think about it."

> **A SURVIVOR SPEAKS**
>
> *"I was just driving along and a Beetles song titled 'In My Life' came on, and I just burst out in tears and had to pull over to the side of the road. I have learned that happens to me and to be kind to myself when it does."*

"Time heals all wounds."

"God wouldn't give you anything more than you can bear."

"It could be worse."

These and other clichés are harmful to grievers because they essentially minimize or try to shut down your normal grief. And when this happens, it might make you feel a little crazy because everyone's telling you one thing while your internal reality is completely the opposite.

In addition to saying unempathetic things, some people around you may at times do hurtful things as well. They might avoid you or pretend nothing's wrong. They might become inappropriately, selfishly emotional in your presence, forcing you to comfort them instead of the other way around. They might give you an insensitive gift. They might blame you or put more of a burden on you in some way through their actions. And when such things happen, you might feel like it's your instinctual reaction to what they've done that's wrong.

Just remember that when it comes to grief, it's our culture that's crazy, not you. And that's why people so often say and do hurtful things to grievers—because the culture is generally not teaching them loss-related emotional intelligence. However, most of these people are well-intentioned so we sometimes have to take a deep breath and remind ourselves to have grace. They know not what they do.

EXPRESS YOURSELF:
Go to *The Understanding Your Suicide Grief Journal* on p. 134.

You're Not Crazy, You're Grieving

Never forget that your journey through the wilderness of your suicide grief may bring you through all kinds of strange and unfamiliar terrain. As I said at the beginning of this touchstone, your experiences may feel so alien that you feel more like you're on the moon! When you feel like you're going crazy, remind yourself to look for the trail marker that assures you you're not going crazy. You're grieving. The two can feel remarkably similar sometimes. For more information on this topic, see my book *You're Not Crazy - You're Grieving: 6 Steps for Surviving Loss.*

And now in Touchstone Seven let's turn to how to best nurture yourself during this naturally difficult time.

Nurture Yourself

Again, the word "bereaved," which to our modern-day ears can sound like an old-fashioned term, means "to be torn apart" and "to have unique needs." Perhaps your most important need right now is to be compassionate with yourself. In fact, the word "compassion" means "with empathy." Caring for and about yourself with great empathy is self-compassion.

> "Getting better means being patient with oneself when progress is slow... It means finding safe, supportive persons with whom to share the pain."
>
> – Janice Harris Lord

This touchstone is a gentle reminder to be kind to yourself as you journey through the wilderness of your grief. If you were embarking on a hike of many days through the rugged, high-altitude mountains of Colorado, would you dress scantily, carry little water, and push yourself until you dropped? Of course not. You would prepare carefully and proceed cautiously. You would take care of yourself because if you didn't, you could die. The consequences of not taking care of yourself in grief can be equally devastating.

Yet over many years of walking with people in suicide grief, I have discovered that most of us are at risk for being hard on ourselves when we're in mourning. We judge ourselves and we shame ourselves and we take care of ourselves last. But good self-care is essential to your survival. To practice good self-care doesn't mean you're feeling sorry for yourself or being self-indulgent; rather, it means you're creating conditions that allow you to integrate the death of someone loved into your heart and soul.

I believe that it is only in nurturing ourselves, in allowing ourselves the time and loving attention we need to journey safely and deeply through grief, that we can find meaning in our continued living. We have all heard the words, "Blessed are those who mourn, for they shall be comforted." To this I might add, "Blessed are those who learn self-compassion during times of grief, for they shall go on to discover continued meaning in life, living, and loving."

Remember—self-care fortifies your long and challenging grief journey, a journey that leaves you profoundly affected and deeply changed. To be self-nurturing is to have the courage to pay attention to and honor your needs. Above all, self-nurturing is about self-acceptance. When we recognize that grief care begins with ourselves, we no longer think of those around us as being responsible for our well-being. Healthy self-care forces us to mourn in ways that help us heal, and that is nurturing indeed.

I also believe that self-nurturing is about taking time to enjoy the moment, to find hidden treasures where you can—a child's smile, a beautiful sunrise, a flower in bloom, a friend's gentle touch. Grief teaches us the importance of living fully in the present while also remembering our past and embracing our future.

EXPRESS YOURSELF:
Go to *The Understanding Your Suicide Grief Journal* on pp. 136-137.

Nurturing Your Whole Self

We tend to think of grief as an emotional experience. It is indeed that, but it's more than that. The profound grief that follows the death of someone to suicide affects us physically, cognitively, emotionally, socially, and spiritually. In other words, grief is a holistic experience, which means when we are grieving, our self-care must also be holistic.

What follows is a brief introduction to caring for each of these facets of your self. You will then be invited to go to your companion journal and express how you see yourself doing in each of these areas.

NURTURING YOURSELF PHYSICALLY

As you're journeying through grief, your body may be letting you know it feels distressed. Actually, one literal definition of the word "grievous" is "causing physical suffering." You may be shocked by how much your body responds to the impact of your loss.

Among the most common physical responses to loss are troubles with sleeping and low energy. You may have difficulty getting to sleep. Perhaps even more commonly, you may be waking up early in the morning and having trouble getting back to sleep. The problem is, when you're grieving your body needs more rest than usual, not less. In general, you may find yourself tiring more quickly— sometimes even at the start of the day. This is called the lethargy of grief, and it's a natural mechanism intended to slow you down and encourage you to care for your body.

But even if you're fatigued, you may not be sleeping well. Many people in grief experience sleep disturbance. If you think about it, sleeping is a primary way in which we routinely release control. But when someone in your life dies by suicide, you naturally feel a loss of control. You may not want to lose any more control by sleeping. The need to stay awake may also relate to the fear of additional losses. If you stay awake and vigilant, you may feel you can help prevent more loss. Some grieving people have even taught me that they stay awake hoping to not miss the person who died in case they return or offer a sign. All of these sleep-depriving rationales— whether they're conscious or unconcious—are normal and understandable.

You may also feel unwell. Muscle aches and pains, shortness of breath, feelings of emptiness in your stomach, tightness in your throat or chest, digestive problems, sensitivity to noise, heart palpitations, queasiness, nausea, headaches, increased allergic reactions, changes in appetite, weight loss or gain, agitation, and generalized tension—these are all ways your body may react to the death.

What's more, if you have a chronic existing health issue, it may become worse. The stress of grief can suppress your immune system, elevate stress chemicals like cortisol, and make you more susceptible to physical problems.

Right now you may not feel in control of how your body is responding, but keep in mind that it's communicating with you about the stress you're experiencing. Most of the time, the physical symptoms we have been reviewing here are normal and temporary.

Still, good physical self-care is important at this time. Your body is the house you live in. Just as your house requires care and maintenance to protect you from the outside elements, your body requires that you honor it and treat it with respect. The quality of your life ahead depends on how you take care of your body today. This includes openly expressing your grief. Many grieving people have taught me that if they avoid or repress talking about the death, their bodies begin to express their grief for them.

IDEAS FOR PHYSICAL SELF-CARE

Stay Fluid

When you experience grief and loss, the mechanism in your body that lets you know when you are thirsty often shuts down. So, you will be well served to remind yourself to drink lots of water—at least six to eight tall glasses every day. Think of water as the oil that lubricates the body. Water (I often call it the very best fluid in the world) carries oxygen, nutrients, and hormones to your cells and eliminates waste products via the bloodstream and your lymphatic system. Remaining well hydrated also means having better digestion and less dry skin. Also, keep in mind that caffeinated and alcoholic drinks dehydrate you, so consider eliminating or limiting your intake.

Rest, Relax, and Renew

To experience grief invites you to suspend and slow down, not speed up and keep busy. So, right now you need to build in time each day to experience some rest, relaxation, and renewal. Some people might tell you to keep busy, but odds are your body will try to tell you to slow down. You might also think you don't have time to do this, but right now, with your very unique needs, you need to make time! Rest helps your body survive right now and helps begin to restore your spirit. So, stop "doing" and simply "be" as much as you possibly can.

Try to Sleep as Well as Possible

No doubt your normal sleep-pattern is disturbed right now. You are probably falling asleep only when totally exhausted and then waking up throughout the night. This is much more common for suicide loss survivors than sleeping normally. Your "sleep rhythm" is thrown off. As you mourn this will improve, but don't think there is something wrong with you because you are not sleeping as you normally have in the past. Sleep is restorative, and if anyone needs restoration right now it is you. So, try the best you can to get some sleep and use tools to assist you in the process. For example, try to get to bed at a similar time each night and get up at a similar time each morning. Limit your caffeine and alcohol intake. If you're getting very little sleep or none at all, see your primary care provider immediately. You need energy to do the work of mourning, and if you are not getting any sleep, you will be grieving but not mourning.

Have a Compassionate Physician as Part of Your Self-Care Plan

As noted, your body is very vulnerable right now. You will be wise to have a caring physician who can help you monitor your physical needs. He or she can assist you in monitoring what your body is telling you about the demand it is experiencing. Be sure to tell your physician about the death; it is critical information if he or she is to be able to help you at this time. Think of your physician as a kind of coach—a trained professional—who can help you care for your body that houses your spirit. He or she can also be an "encourager" during this difficult time in your life. Ask your physician to help you establish some form of daily exercise plan that will help have a calming effect on your body, mind, and spirit. If you don't already have a trusted physician in your corner, get some help finding one right now and work to create a health-partnership.

Laugh When You Have an Opportunity

It turns out that humor is good medicine for your body, mind, and spirit. Research demonstrates that laughter stimulates chemicals in the brain that actually suppress stress-related hormones. Also, respiration and circulation are both enhanced through laughter.

In your grief, you may not feel like laughing very much right now. But as the journey progresses, find ways to build laughter into your life. You might rent a movie that brings a smile to your face or spend time with a friend that lightens your heart.

I hope the above guidelines related to physical self-care will help you take good care of your health. Knowing more about the needs of your body can help you design a program that best meets your unique needs. A personal commitment to your health paves the way for healthy self-care in the other four areas outlined below. Just as your life is being transformed right now, you can also transform your body and re-ignite your divine spark—that which gives your life meaning and purpose.

EXPRESS YOURSELF:
Go to *The Understanding Your Suicide Grief Journal* on pp. 138-139.

NURTURING YOURSELF COGNITIVELY

Your mind gives you the intellectual capacity to think, absorb information, make decisions, and reason logically. Without a doubt, this capacity has also been temporarily affected by your grief. Just as your body and emotions are letting you know you've been torn apart by this loss, your mind has also, in effect, been torn apart.

Thinking normally after the death of someone precious to you would be very unlikely. Don't be surprised if you struggle with short-term memory problems, are finding it hard to focus or concentrate, have trouble making even simple decisions, or think you may be going crazy. Essentially, your mind is in a state of shock, disorientation, and confusion.

Early in your grief, you may find it helpful to allow yourself to suspend all thought and purposefulness for a time. Allow yourself just to be. Your mind needs time to catch up with and process your new reality. In the meantime, don't expect too much from your cognitive self.

DIVINE SPARK

Your divine spark is the still, small voice inside you that knows your meaning and purpose. It is your spiritual core. It is the glow of your soul within you. It is your deepest, truest self.

Your divine spark has been naturally impacted by grief. You relight it by mourning authentically. You eventually strengthen it by nurturing your spirit and feeding it with wonder, joy, gratitude, congruence, meaning, and love.

IDEAS FOR COGNITIVE SELF-CARE

Following are just a few ideas to get you thinking about what helps you feel cognitively well cared for. Whatever those things are, be sure to build at least one or two into each day.

Ask yourself two questions: What do I want? What is wanted of me? The answers to these questions may help you not only survive the coming months and years but learn to love life again.

First, now that the person has died by suicide, what do you want? What do you want to do with your time? What do you not want to do with your time? Where do you want to live? With whom do you want to socialize? Whom do you want to be near? These are big questions that may take some time for you to contemplate and answer.

Second, what is wanted of you? Who needs you? Who depends upon you? What skills and experience can you bring to others? What are you good at? Why were you put here on this earth? While considering what you want is important, it alone does not make a complete life.

On a more practical level, asking yourself these questions at the start of each day may help you focus on the here-and-now and set your intention one day at a time. What do I want from my life today? What is wanted of me today? Living in the moment through daily intention-setting will help you better cope with your grief.

Make a list of goals

While you shouldn't set a particular time and course for your healing, it may help you to make other life goals for the coming year. Consider writing a list of short-term goals for the next three months. Maybe some of the goals could have to do with mourning activities (for example, making a memory book or writing thank-you notes to people who helped at the time of the death).

Also consider making a separate list of long-term goals for the next year. Be both realistic and compassionate with yourself as you consider what's feasible and feels good and what will only add more unneeded stress to your life. Keep in mind that because of your grief, you may continue to feel more fatigued than usual. Don't overcommit, thereby setting yourself up for failure. And try to include at least one or two just-for-fun goals on this list. For example, you might want to take a class or get started on a small, enjoyable project.

If at all possible, avoid making any major changes in your life for at least two years

While it can be helpful to have goals to help you look to a brighter future, it's a mistake to march too boldly ahead. Sometimes, in an effort to obliterate the pain and "move on," mourners make rash decisions shortly after a death. Some move to a new home or city. Some quit their jobs. Some break ties with people in their life or take on new relationships too quickly. Typically these changes are soon regretted. They often end up compounding feelings of loss and complicating healing as well as creating staggering new headaches. You cannot run away from the pain, so don't make things worse by trying to. Instead, give yourself at least a full twenty-four months to consider any other major changes in your life.

Of course, sometimes you may be forced to make a significant change in your life soon after a death. Financial realities may force you to sell your house or relocate, for example. In these cases, know that you're doing what you must and trust that everything will work out.

Have gratitude

You may not be feeling very good about your life right now. You may feel that you're unlucky. You may feel you're destined to be unhappy or lonely. You may feel that the universe is conspiring against you. If you've been having any of these feelings, it's OK. There is, indeed, a time for everything—including self-doubt, self-pity, and a sense of injustice. Indeed, they can be as normal a part of your grief as anger or sadness. Be assured, your life has purpose and meaning, even without the presence of the person who died by suicide. It will just take you some time to think and feel this through for yourself and to actively mourn as you journey through the wilderness of your grief.

When you have the energy to do so, I hope you will purposefully think of all you have to be grateful for, both in your past and your present. This is not to deny the hurt, for the hurt needs to take precedence right now. But when the timing is right, it will also help to consider the things that make your life worth living.

EXPRESS YOURSELF:

Go to *The Understanding Your Suicide Grief Journal* on pp. 140-142.

TUNING INTO YOUR LOVE LANGUAGE

In his landmark 1995 book The Five Love Languages, author Dr. Gary Chapman introduced the idea that human beings feel cared for by others in five primary ways:

1. Receiving gifts

2. Spending quality time together

3. Hearing words of affirmation

4. Being the beneficiary of acts of service

5. Experiencing physical touch

What's your preferred love language? Becoming aware of which love language makes you feel best cared for and encouraging your friends and family members to support you by using it will help you feel nurtured and understood in your grief. You can even use your own preferred love language on yourself as you care for yourself physically, cognitively, emotionally, socially, and spiritually.

NURTURING YOURSELF EMOTIONALLY

In Touchstone Four we explored a multitude of emotions that are common in grief and mourning. These symptoms signal that you have unique needs right now—needs that require your own attention as well as the attention and support of others. Acknowledging and becoming familiar with the terrain of these emotions and practicing good emotional self-care can and will help you authentically mourn and heal in small doses over time.

The important thing to remember is that when we pay attention to our feelings, we honor them. Whenever a grief feeling arises, I encourage you to notice it and let it absorb your full attention for at least a few minutes. Remember—it's another facet of your love for the person who died, and it's there for a reason. It's trying to teach you something about the story of your loss or your needs moving forward. Name the feeling when you're ready. Ask it where it came from and what else it's connected to.

Embracing and befriending your feelings in this way acknowledges their right to be there and over time helps them soften. As they soften, they can better integrate with all the other feelings and experiences in your life. Instead of commanding all your heart and attention, they become part of the unique and precious tapestry that is your life.

IDEAS FOR EMOTIONAL SELF-CARE

In addition to mourning openly and honestly, which gives your normal and necessary grief feelings their due, I hope you will treat your wounded emotions with tender loving care. You're hurting. You're suffering. And while the suffering is a natural part of your love, it deserves self-compassion. Be kind to yourself in whatever ways help you feel soothed, comforted, and appropriately indulged. What those ways are will vary widely from person to person.

Following are just a few ideas to get you thinking about what helps you feel emotionally well cared for. Whatever those things are, be sure to build at least one or two into each day.

Reach out and touch

For many people, physical contact with another human being is comforting. In fact, it's one of the five love languages (see p. 189). That's because touch has bodily effects. When we are touched in comforting ways, our brains are flooded with dopamine, serotonin, and oxytocin. These feel-good hormones help regulate our mood and make us feel calmer and happier. What's more, touch stimulates the vagus nerve, which branches out throughout our entire bodies. Its role is to calm the nervous system, which in turn helps boost our immune systems and can lower our blood pressure and heart rate.

Have you hugged anyone lately? Held someone's hand? Put your arm around another human being? Hug someone you feel safe with. Kiss your children or a friend's baby. Walk arm in arm with a neighbor. If you are soothed by touch, you might also appreciate massage, reiki, or another type of touch therapy. Try a session and see how it feels for you.

Listen to music

Listening to music can be very cathartic for mourners because it helps us access the full range of our feelings. Music can soothe the spirit and nurture the heart. All types of music can be healing—rock & roll, classical, blues, folk. Do you play an instrument or sing?

Allow yourself the time to try these activities soon. What music reminds you of the person who died? At first, listening to this special music may be too painful. But later you may find that playing music that reminds you of the person who died helps you befriend your grief and keep them alive in your heart.

Draw a "grief map"

The death of someone to suicide has no doubt stirred up all kinds of thoughts and feelings inside you. Sometimes, corralling all these varied thoughts and feelings in one place can make them feel more comprehensible. You could write about them, but you can also draw them out in diagram form.

Start with a blank sheet of paper. Make a large circle at the center and label it MY GRIEF. This circle represents all your thoughts and feelings since the death. Now draw lines radiating out of this circle and make a smaller bubble at the end of each of these lines. Label each bubble with a thought or feeling that has been part of your grief journey. For example, you might write ANGER in one of the bubbles. Next to the word "anger," jot down notes about why you have felt angry or what this feeling has been like for you. Do this for all your prominent thoughts and feelings.

Your grief map needn't look pretty or follow any certain rules. The most important thing is the process of creating it because it's an effective mourning activity. When you're finished, explain it to someone who cares about you.

Schedule something that gives you pleasure each and every day
Often mourners need something to look forward to, a reason to get out of bed each morning. It can be hard to anticipate the next day when you know you'll be experiencing pain and sadness. To counterbalance your normal and necessary grief, plan to do something you enjoy each day. Reading, baking, going for a walk, shooting hoops, having lunch with a friend, gardening, playing video games—it doesn't matter what it is as long as it gives you emotional respite and helps you feel comforted and soothed for a while.

EXPRESS YOURSELF:
Go to *The Understanding Your Suicide Grief Journal* on pp. 142-145.

NURTURING YOURSELF SOCIALLY

The death of someone you love has probably resulted in a very real sense of disconnection from the world around you. When you reach out to your family and friends, you are beginning to reconnect. By working to become and stay aware of the larger picture—one that includes all of the people in your life—you gain some perspective. You recognize you are part of a greater whole, and that recognition can empower you. You open up your heart to love again and be loved in return when you reach out to others. Your link to family, friends, and community is vital for your sense of wellbeing and belonging.

If you don't nurture the warm, kind relationships that still exist in your life, you will probably continue to feel disconnected and isolated. You may even withdraw into your own little cave in the wilderness and continue to grieve but not mourn. Isolation can then become the barrier that keeps you stuck in the wilderness and prevents your grief from softening over time. If this happens, you will begin to die while you are still alive. So allow your friends and family to nurture you. Let them in and rejoice in the connection. And if you have to be the one to reach out and strengthen connections, that's OK, too. You will find that it is worth every bit of the effort.

IDEAS FOR SOCIAL SELF-CARE

Following are just a few ideas to get you thinking about what helps you feel socially well cared for. Whatever those things are, be sure to build at least one or two into each day.

Recognize that your friendships will probably change

Mourners often tell me how surprised and hurt they feel when friends fall away after a death. This can be particularly true after a suicide death. "I found out who my friends really are," they say. Know that just as you are doing the best you can right now, your friends are doing the best they can, too—even if it doesn't seem that way. Unfortunately, suicide makes some people feel very awkward and uncomfortable. This naturally affects their ability to be of support to you.

The best way for you to respond in the face of faltering friendships is to be proactive and honest. Even though you're the one who's grieving, you may need to be the one to phone your friends and keep in touch. When you do talk to them, be honest. Tell them how you're truly feeling and that you need and appreciate their support. If you find that certain friends can't handle your grief talk, try sticking to lighter topics with them and lean more heavily on the friends who can be present to whatever you're experiencing.

Over time, you will probably notice a natural attrition among your friends. Some may fade away and never come back. You will need to grieve these losses, though you will likely also find that other friendships deepen and new ones emerge.

By contrast, maybe you are one of the fortunate people who feel tremendous support and love from your family and friends after the death of someone loved. If so, rejoice that you have such wise and wonderful companions in your life, and when opportunites arise, offer them the same empathy and presence in return.

Find a grief "buddy"

Though no one else will grieve this death just like you, there are often many others who have had similar experiences. We are rarely totally alone in the wilderness of grief. Even when there is no guide, there are fellow travelers.

Consider finding a grief "buddy"—someone who is also mourning a suicide death, someone you can talk to, someone who also needs a companion in grief right now. You might ask a grieving friend, neighbor, or colleague to join you, or you might find a grief buddy at a suicide grief support group. Make a pact with your grief buddy to call each other whenever one of you needs to talk. Promise to listen to one another without judgment. Commit to spending time together. You might arrange to meet once a week for breakfast or lunch with your grief buddy.

Remember others who had a special relationship with the person who died

At times your appropriately inward focus will make you feel alone in your grief. But you're not alone. There are probably a number of people who cared about and miss the person who died. Think about others who were affected by the death: friends, neighbors, coworkers, distant relatives, caregivers. Is there someone outside of the primary circle of mourners who may be struggling with this death? Perhaps you could call them and experience mutual support.

Or write and mail a brief supportive note, or send a text or email. If you aren't a writer, consider giving them a call or stopping by for a visit.

EXPRESS YOURSELF:
Go to *The Understanding Your Suicide Grief Journal* on pp. 145-147.

THE LONELINESS OF GRIEF

Grievers often tell me they feel lonely. They have been shattered, but the people and the world around them carry on as if nothing happened. This disconnect can make them feel isolated and alone. Has this happened to you?

Human beings are social creatures. While each of us is a capable, autonomous individual, we are not meant to exist for very long on our own. We're built to interact with and rely on others. We're built for empathy, connection, and love—especially when we're grieving.

If you're lonely, finding your way through it involves befriending yourself and befriending others. The best way to build bonds with others is through proximity, repetition, and quality time. When you're near someone frequently, you're more likely to develop a strong relationship with them. But another key factor here is quality time, which is time spent with another person in which you're focusing on each other, communicating well, and mutually empathizing.

If your wilderness of grief feels lonely, I urge you to reach out to others and work on building relationships based on proximity, repetition, and quality time. Just one or two close friendships may be enough. For some people, a suicide grief support group can also play a significant role in both supporting you in grief and easing your loneliness.

As a person experiencing grief, you need and deserve connection. Open yourself to others, and make the extra effort. You will be glad you did.

NURTURING YOURSELF SPIRITUALLY

The suicide death of someone in your life becomes part of the mystery and is not something you can quickly and easily understand. When you are torn apart by grief, you may have many spiritual questions for which there are no easy answers: Is there a God? Why me? Will life ever be worth living again? This natural human tendency to search for meaning after a death is why I would encourage all of us grievers to put down "nurture my spirit" at the top of our daily to-do lists.

My own personal source of spirituality anchors me, allowing me to put my life into perspective. For me, spirituality involves a sense of connection to all things in nature, God, and the world at large. In recent years I have intentionally worked on spending more mindful time in nature, being conscious of what I am grateful for, and being fully present to the people I care about when I'm in their company. These types of daily spiritual practices speak to my soul and help me attend to my divine spark.

However, I recognize that for some people, contemplating a spiritual life in the midst of the pain of grief can be difficult. But grief is first and primarily a spiritual journey through the wilderness. To attend to, embrace, and express your grief is itself a spiritual practice— even when you've lost your faith or are struggling to regain meaning and purpose.

If you're unsure of your capacity to connect with your spirituality in life-affirming ways, try simply approaching some of the moments in your day with the openness of a child. Embrace the pleasures that come from the simple sights, smells, sounds, tastes, and textures that greet your senses. Work on being present to and appreciating the now. If you can do this, you'll find yourself rediscovering the essentials within your soul and the spirit of the world around you.

Nurturing your spiritual self not only helps you mourn and heal your grief, it also, over time, invites you to reconnect with the world and the people around you. Your heart opens wider, and your life begins to take on renewed meaning and purpose. You may become filled with compassion for other people, particularly others who have come to know grief. You may find yourself becoming kinder, more gentle, and more forgiving of others as well as yourself.

IDEAS FOR SPIRITUAL SELF-CARE

Following are just a few ideas to get you thinking about what helps you feel spiritually well cared for. Whatever those things are, be sure to build at least one or two into each day.

Create and spend time in a sacred mourning space

Creating a sacred mourning space just for you may be one of the most loving ways you can help yourself heal. Yes, you need the support of other people, but nurturing yourself during difficult times can also involve going to exile for some time each day.

Whether indoors or out, find or make a place for solitude and contemplation. The word contemplate means "to create space for the divine to enter." Think of your space, perhaps a simple corner, room, or nook in your yard, as a place dedicated exclusively to the needs of the soul. Retreat to your space for a few minutes each day and attend to and honor your grief.

Start each new day with a meditation or prayer

For many mourners, waking up in the morning is the hardest part of their day. It's as if each time you awaken, you must confront anew the realization that someone you love is gone.

Starting the day off with tears and a heavy heart, day in and day out, is so draining. Yet it may be a necessary, unavoidable part of your grief journey, especially in the early weeks and months after the death.

Yet, when you emerge from the early days, you may begin to gain the energy to set the tone for your day by praying or meditating first thing in the morning. When you wake up, stretch before getting out of bed or picking up your phone. Feel the blood coursing through your body. Listen to the hum of your consciousness.

Repeat a simple affirmation or prayer to yourself, such as: "Today I will live and love fully. Today I will appreciate my life." You might also offer words of gratitude: "Thank you, God, for giving me this day. Help me to appreciate it, be present to it, and make it count."

Organize a tree planting

Trees represent the beauty, vibrancy, and continuity of life. A specially selected, located, and planted tree in a public place can honor the person who died and serve as a perennial memorial. You might plan a short ceremony for the tree planting. Or, you could ask another family member to help. You might also consider a personalized marker or sign.

For a more private option, plant a tree in your own yard. Consult your local nursery for an appropriate selection. Flowering trees are especially beautiful in the spring. You might also consider a variety of tree that the person who died loved or that reminds you of a place that was special to them.

Visit the great outdoors

For many people it's restorative and energizing to spend time outside. Mourners often find nature's timeless beauty healing. The sound of a birdsong or the awesome presence of an old tree can help put things in perspective.

Go on a nature walk. Or camping. Or canoeing. The farther away from civilization, the better. Mother Earth knows more about kicking back than all the stress-management experts on the planet— and she charges far less.

What was the favorite outdoor getaway of the person who died? It may be as awesome as a mountain peak or as simple as your own backyard. Wherever it is, go there if you can. Sit in quiet contemplation of your relationship. Offer up your thanks for the love you shared. Close your eyes and feel the person's spirit surround you.

Spend time in "Thin Places"

In the Celtic tradition, "thin places" are spots where the separation between the physical word and the spiritual world seems tenuous. They are places where the veil between Heaven and earth, between the holy and the everyday, are so thin that when we are near them, we intuitively sense the timeless, boundless spiritual world. There is a Celtic saying that Heaven and earth are only three feet apart, but in the thin places that distance is even smaller.

Thin places are usually outdoors, often where water and land meet or land and sky come together. You might find thin places on a riverbank, a beach, or a mountaintop. Go to a thin place to pray, to walk, or simply sit in the presence of the holy.

If you find these spiritual practice suggestions helpful, you might also find my book *Healing Your Grieving Soul: 100 Spiritual Practices for Mourners* a useful resource.

EXPRESS YOURSELF:
Go to *The Understanding Your Suicide Grief Journal* on pp. 147-150.

What are You Doing to Take Good Care of Yourself Today?

Good self-care is always important, of course, but when you're in grief it's even more essential. If you're not taking extra-tender care of yourself physically, cognitively, emotionally, socially, and spiritually, you won't have the energy or resources you need to work on the six needs of mourning—which are themselves essential aspects of self-care in grief.

So whenever possible, I hope you will stop whatever you're busy with and take a moment to ask yourself, "What am I doing today to take good care of myself?" If you can devote even a few minutes of time every day to each aspect of self-care, you will be equipping yourself with the basic supplies you need for the journey.

Finding others who will be good to you on your journey is also critically important. You can't walk this path alone. In the next touchstone my hope is to help you construct a plan to reach out to others for help.

Reach Out for Help

You've probably noticed that wild geese fly in formation. Let's consider their wisdom.

When geese fly in a "V" shape, the flapping of the wings of each individual goose results in an uplift for the bird that follows. The entire flock achieves seventy-one percent greater flying range than if each bird flew alone. When the goose leading the flock gets tired, it rotates back into the formation, and another goose assumes the point position. As they fly, the geese also honk to each other by way of encouragement and community.

> *"At times our light goes out and is rekindled by a spark from another person."*
>
> Albert Schweitzer

What's more, if any one goose has a problem while they're in flight, two additional geese will always drop out of formation and follow the wayward goose to the ground to help support and protect it. They remain with the goose with special needs until it can continue the journey. If there is ever a time in life when we need to follow the example of the wild geese, it's when we come to grief.

When someone dies by suicide, we naturally grieve, but we must intentionally mourn if we are to renew our capacity to live and love well. In other words, mourning is what generates healing. As I've been emphasizing, this means we heal by expressing our grief outside of ourselves—bit by bit, day by day—in all the ways we find helpful.

But it also means we heal by getting affirmation and empathy from other people all along the way. Remember, the sixth need of mourning is to receive help from others—now and always. Healing requires the support and understanding of those around you as you work on the other five needs of mourning. Healing requires paying heed to the instinctual wisdom of geese.

I've said that the wilderness of your grief is your wilderness and that it's up to you to find your way through it. That's true. But paradoxically, you also need companionship as you journey. You need people who will walk beside you and help provide you with divine momentum. You do not need people who want to walk in front of you and lead you down the path they think is right, nor do you need people who want to walk behind you and not be present to your pain.

You've heard me urge you a number of times in this book to seek out the support of the people in your life who are naturally good helpers. A few shoulders to cry on and some compassionate listening ears can make all the difference in the world.

I also want you to note that this touchstone is titled "Reach Out for Help" and not "Wait Around for Others to Reach Out to You." While you might be wishing your friends and family would be frequently stopping by, calling, texting, inviting you over for dinner, etc., unfortunately this may not be the case. So if you're not getting the support you need, the most self-compassionate thing you can do is to be proactive in seeking that support. Remember how we talked about setting your intention to heal and cultivating spiritual optimism? Reaching out to others is a critical part of this self-empowering approach to integrating this profound loss into your life.

It's true that sharing your pain with others won't make it disappear. You have probably learned that already. However, it will, over time, make it more bearable. What's more, reaching out for help also connects you to other people and strengthens the bonds of love that make life seem worth living. Think of the connections in your life as the mat on a trampoline. The people who support you in grief both cradle you—supporting you and helping prevent you from sinking into despair—and as you do the hard work of mourning, lift you up, eventually creating a springboard to meaning and purpose, love and joy.

EXPRESS YOURSELF:
Go to *The Understanding Your Suicide Grief Journal* on pp. 152-153.

Where to Turn for Help

"There is strength in numbers," one saying goes. Another echoes, "United we stand, divided we fall." If you are grieving, you will indeed find strength and a sense of stability if you draw on an entire support system for help.

While friends and family members can often form the core of your support system, that is not always the case. Seek out people who encourage you to be yourself and who acknowledge your many thoughts and feelings about the death. What you need most now are caring, nonjudgmental listeners.

You may also find comfort in talking to a spiritual leader. When someone dies by suicide, it's natural for you to feel ambivalent about your beliefs and question the very meaning of life. If you belong to a faith tradition, you may want to make an appointment with a leader at your church, temple, mosque, or other place of worship. If your spiritual beliefs are more eclectic or secular, you might find it helpful to talk to a humanist clergyperson or seeker dedicated to spiritual growth and higher consciousness. You might even have friends who are spiritually grounded mentors. Someone who responds not with criticism but with empathy to all your feelings can be a valuable resource.

For many suicide loss survivors, support groups are one of the best helping resources. In a group of fellow mourners, you can connect with others who have also experienced suicide death and may have similar thoughts and feelings. You will be allowed and gently encouraged to talk about the person who died as much and as often as you like.

A professional grief-informed counselor may also be a very helpful addition to your support system. In fact, a trained counselor can be something friends and family members often can't—an objective listener. A counselor's office can be that safe haven where you can let go of any feelings you're afraid to express elsewhere. What's more, a good counselor will then help you constructively channel those emotions. Remember, help comes in different forms for different people. The trick is to find the combination that works best for you and then make use of it.

EXPRESS YOURSELF:
Go to *The Understanding Your Suicide Grief Journal* on pp. 154-155.

Rule of Thirds

In my own grief journeys and in the lives of the mourners I have been privileged to counsel, I have discovered that in general, you can take all the people in your life and divide them into thirds when it comes to grief support.

About a third of the people in your life will turn out to be neutral in response to your grief. While they may still be good companions for non-grief-related activities in your life, they are not equipped to be empathetic grief supporters. Or they may say, "If you need me, just let me know"—but then you won't hear from them again. They will neither help nor hinder you in your journey.

Another third of the people in your life will be harmful to you in your efforts to mourn and heal. While they are usually not setting out to intentionally harm you, they will judge you, they will shame you, they will try to take your grief away from you, and they will pull you off the path to healing. You will feel worse after you spend time in their company. Stay away from them as much as you can for now. Consciously or unconsciously, they will trip you up and cause you to stumble and fall.

But here's the good news: the final third of the people in your life will turn out to be truly empathetic helpers. They will have a desire to understand you and your unique thoughts and feelings about the death. They will demonstrate a willingness to be taught by you and a recognition that you are the expert of your experience, not them. They will be willing to bear witness to your pain and suffering without feeling the need to take it away from you. They will believe in your capacity to heal.

While you may find that the people in your life divide up into different proportions than thirds, seek out the friends and family members who fall into this last group. They will be your confidants and momentum-givers on your journey.

EXPRESS YOURSELF:
Go to *The Understanding Your Suicide Grief Journal* on p. 155.

How Others Can Help You: Three Essentials

While there are a multitude of ways that other people can help you in your grief, here are three important and fundamental helping goals. Effective helpers will help you:

1. Encounter your loss

These are the people who understand the need for you to revisit and recount the pain of your loss. They help you tell your story and provide a safe place for you to openly mourn. Essentially, they give you an invitation to take the grief that is inside you and share it with them.

2. Feel companioned on your journey

These people serve as companions no matter what you're thinking or feeling on any given day. They know that extending true empathy means walking with you on the journey, not ahead of you or behind you. One of the meanings of the word "grieve" is "to bear a heavy burden." Those who companion you in your grief realize that as they help bear your burden of sorrow, they shoulder some of the weight, and they help you trust that you'll eventually come out of the dark and into the light.

3. Embrace hope

These are the people you know who help you feel hopeful. They sustain the presence of hope as you feel separated from those things that make life worth living. They have so much hope, you can often even borrow some of theirs. They can be present to you in your loss yet bring you a sense of trust in yourself that you can and will heal.

EXPRESS YOURSELF:
Go to *The Understanding Your Suicide Grief Journal* on p. 156.

SUICIDE IN THE MILITARY

Many military families are impacted by suicide (both active duty and veterans). Obviously, there needs to be a focus not just on prevention and intervention, but also on providing support to suicide loss survivors.

Service members and veterans who are in crisis or having thoughts of suicide, and those who know a service member or a veteran in crisis, can call the Veteran/Military Crisis Line for confidential support available 24 hours a day, 7 days a week, 365 days a year. Call 988 and press "1", text 838225, or chat online at MilitaryCrisistLine.net.

A valuable source of support for military suicide loss survivors is the Tragedy Assistance Program for Survivors (TAPS) . They have supported tens of thousands of military suicide loss survivors by offering hope and connection. Contact them at www.taps.org/suicide.

Reaching Out to a Support Group

For some people, grief support groups, where people come together and share the common bond of experience, can be invaluable in helping them heal. In these groups, each person can share their unique grief journey in a nonthreatening, safe atmosphere. Group leaders and members are usually very patient with you and your grief and understand your need for support long after the death.

For some mourners, grief support groups form the core of their support systems. If your friends and family lack the capacity to provide you with sufficient support beyond the early days of grief, a good support group can help fill the gap. It's also important to keep in mind that those closest to you may understandably grow grief-fatigued in the months to come. Even if you have exceptionally empathetic and supportive family and friends, you will probably find that grief support group members can better sustain their focus on your grief (and you on theirs) over the longer term.

You might think of grief support groups as places where fellow journeyers gather. Each of you has a story to tell. Your dispatches from the wilderness help affirm the normalcy of each other's experiences. You also help each other build divine momentum toward healing.

EXPRESS YOURSELF:
Go to *The Understanding Your Suicide Grief Journal* on p. 156.

HOW TO FIND A SUPPORT GROUP

To find a suicide support group in your area, contact the American Association of Suicidology at 1-202-237-2280 or go to their website at www.suicidology.org. Another contact option is the American Foundation for Suicide Prevention at 1-888-333-2377 or go to their website at www.afsp.org. Googling "suicide grief support groups near me" is another way to find options that may work for you.

Perhaps you are interested in joining an online grief support group. This can be particularly effective if you're comfortable communicating online and would like to meet others who have also experienced a loss to suicide.

I also believe that for your first grief support group experience, it's best to participate in a closed-ended group with set starting and ending dates. In these types of groups, professionals or trained lay facilitators usually provide some education about grief (typically by using a book such as this one) as well as time for open discussion and sharing. Members come together for a fixed number of sessions. Everyone starts and stops at the same time, often meeting

GETTING HELP IN A CRISIS

If your grief is ever so overwhelming that your life or the life of someone in your care is in danger, you are in crisis and should seek help immediately.

Signs of a crisis include:

• Thinking about, planning, or attempting suicide

• Failing to care for yourself (e.g., eating, bathing, dressing)

• Abusing alcohol or drugs

If any of these warning signs apply to you, reach out to one of the helping resources below without delay.

Call your counselor
Call your primary-care provider
Call 911
Call 988
Call the National Suicide Prevention Lifeline: 800-273-TALK (8255) or use the live online chat at suicidepreventionlifeline.org/chat
Text the National Crisis Text Line: text HOME to 741741 (U.S. and Canada)
Call your local emergency room

once a week for a period of several months. People are not joining or leaving the group midstream.

This type of group gives members a strong foundation of basic grief and mourning principles that will help them embark on a healthy path through the wilderness and maintain momentum long after the group has ended. What's more, members have the chance to meet, bond, and graduate together. This creates a strong, cohesive group dynamic.

After this closed group has ended, it's common for now-bonded members to continue to meet regularly for more informal support and possibly join up with past graduates of the same initial support group experience. This type of open-ended, less structured, ongoing group can be a wonderful source of long-term support. However, in my experience, an effective way to get started is in a closed-ended group that combines education with ongoing support.

In the beginning of your journey, you may not feel ready for a support group. It's common for shock, numbness, and other early grief responses to make it difficult for some mourners to participate in or feel helped by a support group. If this is where you find yourself, it's OK to postpone joining a group for a while and in the meantime, get individual support from a grief counselor instead. However, do keep in mind, that some suicide loss survivors find it very helpful to seek out support groups early on in their experience. If you are uncertain about participating in the support group, it can be wise to reach out to group leaders to determine if it's an appropriate avenue of support for your needs at this time. It's also OK to repeat the introductory grief group if after graduation you realize you were too psychically numb to have fully benefited from it.

Finally, keep in mind that grief support sources can be combined. For example, you may want to see a counselor while you are participating in a support group as well. Such tandem approaches are needed for some grievers to feel adequately supported.

EXPRESS YOURSELF:
Go to *The Understanding Your Suicide Grief Journal* on p. 157.

HOW TO KNOW IF YOU'VE FOUND A HELPFUL SUPPORT GROUP
Not all support groups will be helpful to you. Sometimes the group dynamic becomes unhealthy for one reason or another. Look for the following signs of a healthy support group.

1.   Group members acknowledge that each person's grief is unique.

They respect and accept both what members have in common and what is unique to each person.

2. Group members understand that grief is not a disease but instead a normal process without a specific timetable or sequential steps.

3. All group members are encouraged to talk about their grief. However, if some decide to listen without sharing, their preference is respected.

4. Group members understand the difference between actively listening to what another person is saying and expressing their own thoughts and feelings. They make every effort not to interrupt when someone else is speaking.

5. Group members respect one another's right to confidentiality. Thoughts, feelings, and experiences shared in the group are not made public or shared with anyone else outside the group.

6. Each group member is allowed equal time to speak; one or two people do not monopolize the group's time.

7. Group members don't give advice to each other unless it's asked for.

8. Group members recognize that thoughts and feelings are neither right nor wrong. They listen with empathy to the thoughts and feelings of others without trying to change them.

9. The group leaders have gone through training experiences that help them in their facilitator roles.

10. The group leaders can provide referrals for additional support when that is appropriate.

EXPRESS YOURSELF:
Go to *The Understanding Your Suicide Grief Journal* on pp. 157-158.

REACHING OUT TO A GRIEF COUNSELOR
I believe that individual counseling is an excellent addition to any griever's self-care plan. In the Introduction (see page 15), I covered the concept of "companioning," which is the grief-counseling philosophy I created and teach to other caregivers. A compassionate grief companion will help you feel seen, heard, affirmed, and understood. What's more, if you're feeling like you're

---

MOURNING CARRIED GRIEF

If you've suffered past losses in your life, it's common for those griefs to come up again when a new loss occurs. As you're working your way through this book you may realize that you've never fully and openly mourned some of those past losses. When this happens, it means you're probably carrying old, unreconciled grief.

Carried grief is dangerous because it's a common, invisible, insidious cause of long-term wellness issues that negatively affect your quality of life. In my work with grieving people, I have many times found it to be at the root of struggles with anxiety, depression, challenges with intimacy, risk for substance abuse, and more. It mutes your divine spark, and it causes some people to die while they are alive.

If you think you may be carrying old grief, I urge you to work with a grief counselor to explore and mourn it. Each loss really needs its own consideration, and an effective counselor can help you not only sort out all your intermingled griefs but also create a mourning plan to give each one some dedicated attention. Of course, the counselor will also help you actively and effectively engage with your current grief, as well.

The good news is that engaging with and reconciling longstanding carried grief can be a life-changing process. I've had mourners describe it as "waking up" and "truly living for the first time."

A SURVIVOR SPEAKS

"I had experienced the sudden death of my mother when I was eight years old. After my husband took his own life, it brought it all up for me. No one had ever really helped me mourn the death of my mother. Now, I was confronted with the need to mourn her and my husband."

going crazy or doing grief "wrong," they'll assure you that what you're experiencing is normal.

Grief counseling is simply a form of self-care. I've noticed that some people think of self-care wellness practices such as yoga, massage, and acupuncture as normal parts of routine physical, emotional, and spiritual maintenance, while other people construe them as overly indulgent or superfluous. When it comes to grief counseling (and all forms of self-care), I encourage you to align yourself with the first group. This is your one, precious life. You need and deserve holistic care, and that includes skilled grief care when you are in deep grief.

EXPRESS YOURSELF:
Go to *The Understanding Your Suicide Grief Journal* on p. 158-159.

HOW TO FIND THE RIGHT COUNSELOR FOR YOU

Finding the right counselor to help you through the grief process sometimes takes a little doing. A recommendation from someone you trust is probably the best place to start. If they had a good counseling experience and think you would work well with this counselor, then you might want to make an initial appointment. Ultimately, though, only you will be able to determine if a particular counselor is right for you.

If a friend's recommendation doesn't work out, try contacting:

- Your primary-care provider, who may be able to refer you to a grief-care specialist.

- Local suicide grief support groups, which often maintain a list of counselors.

- A local information and referral service, such as a crisis intervention center, which may maintain a list of counselors who focus on grief work.

- A local hospital, family service agency, funeral home, and/or mental health clinic. Many of which usually maintain a list of referral sources.

- A local hospice, which may even have a counselor on staff who might be available to work with you.

During your first counseling session, consider asking:

- Have you had specialized grief-care training?

- What is your experience working with grieving people?

- What is your counseling approach with a person who has experienced a death by suicide?

Trust your instincts. You may leave your first counseling session feeling you've clicked with the counselor, or it may well take you several sessions to form an opinion. Ultimately, if you feel like a counselor isn't a good fit—for whatever reason—try a different one. It's OK to have an initial consultation with a few counselors before you settle on one.

EXPRESS YOURSELF:
Go to *The Understanding Your Suicide Grief Journal* on pp. 159-160.
LENGTH OF COUNSELING

Some grieving people only need a few sessions, while others benefit from a longer-term counseling relationship. Discuss this issue openly with your counselor and decide what's best for you.

One helpful way to determine an appropriate length of counseling is called a "time contract." With this method, the counselor and you meet for an initial consultation and agree on a certain number of sessions. That number may vary considerably depending on your unique circumstances. At the end of the preestablished number of sessions, the counselor and you decide if more sessions would be helpful. If the time contract idea appeals to you, bring it up with your counselor.

Regardless of the length of your counseling, it's doubtful you'll feel you are easily, steadily moving forward in your grief journey. More likely, the natural ebb and flow of pain and healing will at times make you feel you aren't making steady progress. This is normal. Be patient with yourself as you continue to work on the six needs of mourning.

EXPRESS YOURSELF:
Go to *The Understanding Your Suicide Grief Journal* on p. 160.

Reaching Out When Your Grief is Complicated

In some ways, all grief is complicated. Just as love is always complex and multifaceted, so too is grief. But grief counselors sometimes use the term "complicated grief" to talk about a grief experience that is extra complicated. It's a matter of degree, features, impact on the ability to function in daily life, and sometimes duration.

Complicated grief isn't abnormal or pathological. It's simply normal, necessary grief that has gotten amplified, stuck, or off track somehow. It has encountered barriers or detours of one kind or another and as a result has become stalled, waylaid, or denied altogether.

You might be at risk for complicated grief depending on:

The circumstances of the suicide
Your grief might naturally be complicated secondary to some of the factors outlined in Touchstone 3. You may be well served to give focused attention to those features.

Your personality and mental health
If you are carrying unreconciled grief from previous life losses, or if

you have a tendency toward depression or anxiety, you may be more susceptible to a complicated grief experience. Difficulties in expressing and managing feelings of sadness and anger, extreme dependency on the approval of others, or a tendency to assume too much responsibility may also complicate your grief journey.

Your relationship with the person who died
An intensely close relationship to the person who died can contribute to complicated grief. As can ambivalent relationships and relationships marked by dysfunction, abuse, mental health issues, and separation.

Your capacity to express your grief
If you've been unable to accept the intense emotions evoked by the death, you may experience complicated grief. Or perhaps your family and friends have failed to affirm your feelings of loss. Other significant losses occurring at the same time or the inability to participate in the grief process due to illness or the lack of access to meaningful ceremonies, such as a funeral, can also give rise to complicated grief.

Your use of drugs or alcohol
Drugs or alcohol overuse may suppress your feelings connected with the loss, thus short-circuiting what might otherwise be a normal and healthy grief journey.

Essentially, anything "extra" about a death or other concurrent circumstances in your life heightens the chances of complicated grief. In this book we've talked about grief overload (p. 80), traumatic loss (p. 65), anticipatory grief (p. 67), soulmate grief (p. 70), carried grief (p. 212) and other "whys" that shape your unique grief journey (Touchstone Three). The more extreme and numerous these complicating factors are for you, the more likely you are to naturally find yourself struggling. Everyone's grief wilderness is different. If yours is unusually rugged and harrowing, it's perfectly understandable that you would require additional support.

EXPRESS YOURSELF:
Go to *The Understanding Your Suicide Grief Journal* on p. 161.

CATEGORIES OF COMPLICATED GRIEF

Now and then I talk about complicated grief categories because naming them in this way can sometimes help grievers recognize their own stuck or off-track patterns of grief thoughts, feelings, and behaviors.

Unembarked grief

Unembarked grief is grief that has never been allowed to depart from the trailhead and enter the normal and necessary wilderness of grief. In other words, it is uninitiated or unlaunched grief. Carried grief is a form of unembarked grief. If you feel stuck in shock, numbness, or denial, you may be experiencing unembarked grief.

Impasse grief

Imagine you're hiking through the wilderness and while you're on the trail, you come up against a sheer rock face or a massive downed tree. When you encounter such an obstruction, in order to proceed you must find a way through or around it. Instead, people experiencing impasse grief remain stuck in that particular location. They keep butting up against the same problem. In my counseling experience, the obstruction often comes in the form of a pronounced and prolonged encounter with anger, anxiety, sadness, or guilt that does not soften with time.

Off-trail grief

Sometimes grievers, usually unknowingly, take an unhelpful path. After all, it's not like there's a sign with two arrows, one saying, "Healthy grief this way" and the other, "Caution! Wrong way!" So they embark on or stumble onto a course that occupies them with other tasks and issues in lieu of their normal and necessary grief work. Off-trail grief behaviors are essentially avoidance patterns—habits and behaviors that replace the work of grief and mourning, such as:

- Displacing grief feelings onto another life issue, such as work or relationship issues.

- Replacing the relationship prematurely.

- Focusing on physical symptoms and problems to the exclusion of anything else.

- Getting caught up in addictive behaviors, such as overworking, compulsive shopping, overeating, abusing substances, gambling, overexercising, and more. Essentially, any consuming behavior that thoroughly distracts from the necessary work of grief and mourning.

- Traveling, often to stay on the move in the hopes of outrunning grief.

- Crusading, or over-dedication to or premature involvement with a cause, often related to the circumstances of the suicide death or the passions of the person who died.

Keep in mind that in grief, many of these behaviors can be healthy in moderation and when accompanied by active mourning. If you're exercising a bit more than normal as a means of stress management, for example, that's OK as long as you're also actively encountering your grief and working on the six needs of mourning. It's a question of balance. If you're turning to these behaviors in lieu of attending to your grief and mourning, on the other hand, that's off-trail grief. You may benefit from getting some help from a grief counselor to get back on track.

Encamped grief
Sometimes on the journey through grief, people stop moving—forward, backward, or sideways—and instead step off the trail and set up permanent residence in the wilderness. They build themselves a shelter, unpack provisions, and settle in. These grievers often begin to identify with their loss experience so strongly that they build their new self-identities around the death or the

circumstances of the loss. They "become" their loss story, and it's not uncommon for them to express a sense of pride, loyalty, or honor in their encampment.

If you recognize yourself in any of these complicated grief categories, I don't want you to be alarmed or feel ashamed. They happen all the time, and they're largely products of our mourning-avoidant culture's complicity when it comes to an unhealthy understanding of grief. Instead, I hope you will feel proud of your new insight and motivated to take action to get the extra support you need and deserve. For more on complicated grief, see my book *Complicated Grief: How To Understand, Express, and Reconcile Your Especially Difficult Grief.*

EXPRESS YOURSELF:
Go to *The Understanding Your Suicide Grief Journal* on p. 162.

Getting Help for Complicated Grief

If you feel like you're experiencing complicated grief, you may need some extra help encountering the six needs of mourning. I suggest you might find it beneficial to make an appointment with a grief-informed counselor. Depending on the severity of your symptoms and the degree of difficulty you're having functioning in your daily life, a few sessions may be enough to help you through the most challenging features of the terrain of your wilderness. Or you may need ongoing support for a longer period of time.

Grief counselors can range from therapists to clergy, hospice caregivers, funeral home aftercare staff, and lay-trained caregivers. Grief therapists, on the other hand, have specific clinical training, experience, and interest in grief therapy. For people challenged by complicated grief, I recommend looking for a grief therapist. Your needs will be better met by someone with more in-depth knowledge and experience.

Perhaps it would help to return to the concept of emotional intensive care here. While your primary-care provider's clinic is staffed by highly competent nurses and physicians, it is not the same as an intensive care unit staffed by specially trained acute-care nurses and specialists. Similarly, the appropriate level of care for normal grief is different than the appropriate level of care for complicated grief, although there is certainly a wide gray area in between.

If you're experiencing complicated grief, you have some uniqe needs, and so you need specialized care. Again, if you need help finding a grief therapist, try the same tips for finding a good counselor, on page 213—only this time ask for referrals to therapists who have experience with or specialize in caring for people challenged by complicated grief.

EXPRESS YOURSELF:
Go to *The Understanding Your Suicide Grief Journal* on p. 163.

A Few Last Thoughts about Reaching Out for Help

As a professional grief companion, I have been privileged to have thousands of suicide loss survivors reach out to me for help. Among other important lessons, they've taught me that sharing their grief with others and receiving empathy in return are integral parts of the healing process.

I hope this touchstone has helped you understand the importance of reaching out for help in your grief. Please don't try to confront your grief alone. You need companions—friends, relatives, neighbors, community members, counselors, others who have experienced a suicide loss—who will walk beside you and be your steady companions as you make the difficult journey through the wilderness of your grief.

TOUCHSTONE NINE

Seek Reconciliation,
Not Resolution

How do you ever find your way out of the wilderness of your grief? You don't have to wander there forever, do you?

The good news is that no, you don't have to dwell in deep grief forever. If you follow the trail markers on your journey through the wilderness, if you keep close to the touchstones, you will indeed find your way out.

"Loss has transformed the way I now see, breathe, and feel life. I'll never be the same person again."

Jennifer Ross

A number of psychological grief models talk about "resolution," "recovery," "reestablishment," or "reorganization" as the desired destination of your grief journey. So you might have heard—and may even believe—that your grief journey will end when you resolve, or recover from, your grief.

But you may also be coming to understand one of the fundamental truths of grief: Your journey will never truly, discreetly end. We as humans do not "get over" grief. My personal and professional experience has taught me that a total return to "normalcy" after the death of someone loved is not possible because we are all forever changed by loss. Just as with any significant experience in your life, your journey through the wilderness of grief will become a part of who you are and always live inside you.

"Reconciliation" is the term I find most appropriate for the healing that develops as you work to integrate the loss. We as human beings don't resolve or recover from our grief but instead become reconciled to it.

With reconciliation comes full acknowledgment of the reality of the death. Beyond a cognitive working through of the death, there is also an emotional and spiritual integration. What had been understood at the head level is now understood at the heart level.

Energy and confidence are renewed, and the desire to become reinvolved in the activities of living is reawakened. There is also a deepening wisdom about the fact that pain and grief are difficult, yet necessary, parts of life.

As reconciliation unfolds over time, you will recognize that life is and will continue to be different without the person who died. Changing your relationship with them from one of presence to one of memory and redirecting your energy and initiative toward the future often take longer—and involve more hard work—than most people comprehend before they themselves suffer such a loss.

Keep in mind that if you're still in early survival mode, you might not be ready for this touchstone. If so, it is perfectly OK at this point for you to tuck a bookmark into this page and set down the book for a while. As with all things in grief, you and only you get to decide if and when you are in a place to consider the ideas outlined here.

But keep in mind that reconciliation doesn't just happen. It's an active, intentional process. You reach it through deliberate, authentic mourning, by:

- talking it out.

- crying it out.

- writing it out.

- thinking it out.

- playing it out.

- painting (or sculpting, etc.) it out.

- dancing it out.

- etcetera!

YOUR PATCHWORK HEART

Your heart has been broken, maybe even torn into a million pieces by this suicide death. Active, intentional mourning is the process of stitching it back together.

As you approach reconciliation, your heart will become whole again. But it will be a patchwork heart. The seams where it has been sewn together will always be apparent to you, and they will twinge and ache sometimes. The wounds will be healed, yet the scars will always remain.

But still, in reconciliation you will be able to live wholeheartedly again, because your torn-apart heart will be mended.

To journey toward reconciliation requires that you descend before you can transcend. You don't get to go around or above your grief. You must go through it. And while you are going through it, you must also befriend and express what you are thinking and feeling if you are to truly reconcile yourself to it.

I'm often asked, "How long does grief last?" The hard truth is that grief is forever. As long as you love the person who died, you will continue to grieve them. Like a serious but healed wound on your body, it's always there, but it no longer demands your daily (or hourly or minute by minute) attention. Yes, love does not end. Instead, it learns to live despite the absence.

You will find that as you approach reconciliation, the sharp, ever-present pain of grief will give rise to a renewed sense of meaning and purpose. No, your feelings of loss will never completely disappear, yet they will soften, and the intense pangs of grief will become less frequent. Hope for your continued living will grow as you are able to make commitments to the future, realizing that the person you had a relationship with will never be forgotten. The unfolding of this journey does not return you to an "old normal" but instead leads you to discover a totally new normal.

EXPRESS YOURSELF:
Go to *The Understanding Your Suicide Grief Journal* on pp. 166-167.

Signs of Reconciliation

To help you discern where you are in your movement toward reconciliation at any given time, the following list of signs of integrating this loss into your life may be helpful. However, you don't have to be experiencing all of them for reconciliation to be taking place. In fact, if you're early in the work of mourning, you may not be noticing any of them yet. Be patient and remember that reconciliation is an ongoing, incremental process.

Still, this list may give you a way to keep an eye on your movement through grief. As new reconciliation signs arise, you may even want to place checkmarks next to them. The closer you get to emerging from the wilderness, the more of these signs you will probably notice.

○ A recognition of the reality and finality of the death

○ A return to stable eating and sleeping patterns

○ The enjoyment of experiences in life that are normally enjoyable

○ The establishment of new and healthy relationships

○ The capacity to live a full life without feelings of guilt or lack of self-respect

○ An understanding of the need to organize and plan your life toward the future while always remembering the past

○ The serenity to be comfortable with the way things are rather than attempting to make things as they were

○ The versatility to welcome more change into your life

○ The awareness that you have allowed yourself to authentically, fully grieve and mourn—and you have survived

○ The understanding that you do not "get over" your grief but instead learn to live with the new reality

○ The acquaintance with new parts of yourself that you have discovered in your grief journey

○ The adjustment to new role changes that have resulted from the loss of the relationship

○ The acknowledgment that the pain of loss is intrinsic to the privilege of giving and receiving love

○ A sense of renewed meaning and purpose in your life

Reconciliation emerges much in the way grass grows. We don't typically check our lawns each day to see if the grass is growing, but it does grow, and soon we come to realize it's time to mow the grass again. Likewise, we can't expect to examine our grief movement on a daily or weekly basis to be assured that we're healing. As we've discussed, grief, in the short term, is more of a back-and-forth, round-and-around process. Nonetheless, as long as we're consistently doing the work of mourning, we do eventually realize that over the course of months and years, we've come a long way.

Usually there is not one great moment of "arrival" but instead a series of subtle changes and incremental progress. Along the way, I hope you will stop and take the time to notice and be grateful for even very small advancements. If you're beginning to taste your food again, be thankful. If you mustered the energy to meet a friend for lunch, be grateful. If you finally got a good night's sleep, rejoice.

Here's what C. S. Lewis wrote in *A Grief Observed* about his grief symptoms as they eased in his journey to reconciliation:

"There was no sudden, striking, and emotional transition. Like the warming of a room or the coming of daylight, when you first notice them, they have already been going on for some time."

Of course, the journey toward reconciliation is not an expressway to healing. Even when you're feeling good divine momentum, you're likely to take some steps backward from time to time. That's to be expected. When it happens, be kind to yourself and keep believing in yourself. Set your intention to continue to reconcile your grief, and foster hope that you can and will come to live and love fully again.

EXPRESS YOURSELF:
Go to *The Understanding Your Suicide Grief Journal* on pp. 167-168.

Managing Your Expectations

Movement toward reconciliation in grief is often draining and exhausting. It also can take a very long time. Many grieving people have unrealistic expectations about how readily they should be feeling forward momentum, and when it takes much longer and involves a lot more hard work than they ever imagined, they sometimes experience a loss of self-confidence and self-esteem. They begin to question their capacity to heal. They doubt things will ever get better. They lose hope. If you find yourself in this situation, you're not alone.

If you're feeling doubtful or hopeless, consider if you've consciously or unconsciously set a timetable for reconciliation. Ask yourself questions like, "Have I mistakenly given myself a deadline for when I should be 'over' my grief? Am I expecting myself to heal more quickly than is possible?" If the answer to such questions is yes, recognize that you could be hindering your own healing by expecting too much of yourself too soon. In fact, accepting the pace of your unique journey through your singular wilderness is key to eventual reconciliation. Take your grief and your healing as they come, one day at a time.

One valuable way to make the most of the day-by-day nature of mourning work is to use the companion journal to this book. Write out your many thoughts and feelings, and you will be amazed at how it helps you embrace your grief. But in addition, your journal then becomes a written record of your experience. You can pick it up at any time and reacquaint yourself with your earlier thoughts and feelings. This can help you see the many changes that will have unfolded as you've engaged with the six needs of mourning over the course of your grief journey.

You can't control death or ignore your human need to grieve and mourn when suicide loss impacts your life. You do have the choice, however, to help yourself heal. Embracing and expressing your grief is probably some of the hardest work you will ever do. As you do this work, surround yourself with compassionate, loving people who are willing to walk with you, and try to be unfailingly kind to yourself.

EXPRESS YOURSELF:
Go to *The Understanding Your Suicide Grief Journal* on pp. 168-169.

Not Attached to Outcome

I understand that managing expectations for healing in grief can be difficult. When we're struggling and in pain, it's natural to want to feel better as soon as possible.

Yet reconciling deep grief is not a fast or efficient process. So if we can let go of any expectations for healing quickly or in a certain way, we usually end up suffering less. The practices of accepting what is in each moment and mindfully living as much as possible are what allow us to be present to our grief and our life—which in turn speeds healing and enhances our quality of life.

The concept of nonattachment to outcome applies here. When we take meaningful action without worrying too much about the outcome of that action, we're doing what we can and beyond that, surrendering the illusion of control. Yes, we still can and should intentionally mourn, connect with others, take good care of ourselves, foster hope, and envision our meaningful futures (all activities we can control). But that's where we let go. In short, we act with intention, then what happens, happens.

That's exactly how active, authentic mourning works. If you take meaningful action in doses to work on one or more of the six needs of mourning, you don't need to worry about the outcome of those actions. You can simply trust that over time the mourning will generate divine momentum to carry you toward healing, even if there are lots of ups and downs along the way.

Whenever I have a counseling appointment to see someone who's grieving, right before they're due to arrive, I spend a few minutes in silence repeating this three-phase mantra to myself:

No rewards for speed

Not attached to outcome

Divine momentum

My hope is that as you undertake the long, arduous journey toward reconciliation of your suicide grief, that this same affirmation can be of some support to you.

EXPRESS YOURSELF:
Go to *The Understanding Your Suicide Grief Journal* on p. 170.

Choose Hope for Your Healing

In addition to grief work, permitting yourself to have hope is central to achieving reconciliation. As I've said, hope is trust in a good that is yet to be.

Refusing to give in to despair may by the greatest act of hope there is. Yes, you have gone to the wilderness. Darkness may seem to surround you. But also rising up within you is the profound awareness that the pain of your grief is an inextricable part of the love you shared with the person who died. **Your love is still there. You are still here.**

And so you choose to hope and to work on. Living in the present moment of your pain while having hope for a good that is yet to be are not mutually exclusive. Like grief and love, they coexist, each deepening the experience of the other.

EXPRESS YOURSELF:
Go to *The Understanding Your Suicide Grief Journal* on p. 171.

Borrowing Hope

But what if you don't feel hopeful? What if you're having a hard time mustering hope?

This can happen in grief, and when it does, it's perfectly understandable. Sinking into hopelessness does not mean you're weak or incapable. If you're not suffering from concurrent clinical depression, it simply means your grief may have dipped into a difficult low or may be more complicated—and you need extra support.

As we discussed in the last touchstone, if you're struggling with maintaining hope, you can reach out to a support group or a grief-informed counselor. Those are always good avenues. But you can also borrow hope.

I imagine you know people who exude hope. Some are empathetic listeners, and simply talking to them about your grief can help ease your sense of hopelessness. Others are survivors of a suicide loss, and their wisdom about how it gets better can rekindle your hope. And still others just seem to have hope to spare. They tend to be optimistic, joyful people. Spending time with them can lift your spirits.

On your journey to reconciliation, remember that you can borrow hope if you are ever feeling stalled or stuck. It's a good practice for regaining momentum.

EXPRESS YOURSELF:
Go to *The Understanding Your Suicide Grief Journal* on p. 171.

The Safety Net of Faith

Sometimes in my own journeys through the wilderness of grief, when hope has seemed absent, I have found that faith could sustain me. To me faith can feel like a safety net beneath hope. When hope fails, faith is there to catch me.

You've heard the phrase "blind faith." Actually, that's redundant because all faith is blind. Having faith means believing and trusting in something that has no logical proof or material evidence. I think that the alternative—believing in only what we can see and experience with our five physical senses—is unnecessarily limiting and can deaden our hope and sense of wonder.

On your journey to reconciliation, faith is a bridge that can help you get from your now to your future. Right now your bridge might feel like a wobbly wooden pathway swinging over a great chasm, or it might seem as sturdy and transcendent as the Golden Gate—or somewhere in between. Regardless, to walk your bridge you must put one foot in front of the other, trusting that it will support you.

My own faith is inspired by moments when I'm able to notice the good, sweet, and tender in life, despite the deep wounds of my grief. Stories of the indomitable human spirit give me faith. Opening my heart to the mysteries of spirituality and the universe gives me faith. Your faith may be anchored in religious beliefs or other concepts and experiences. But regardless of the source and nature of your faith, if you lose hope along your journey, I invite you to join me in falling back on faith.

EXPRESS YOURSELF:
Go to *The Understanding Your Suicide Grief Journal* on p. 172.

You Will Get There

If you are just starting out or in the thick of your journey through the wilderness of grief, reconciliation may seem like an impossibly distant destination. It's true that it usually takes a long time and a lot of hard work to get there. But I promise you it's there, waiting for you.

Every day that you authentically encounter and engage with your grief, you're getting one step closer—even if it feels like you're going backward. Each moment you actively work on one of the six needs of mourning, you're getting one step closer. Every time you reach out for help or openly and honestly express your grief, you're getting one step closer.

As long as you are doing the hard work of mourning, you will eventually find meaning and purpose, and your grief will become an integrated part of you. As Anne Lamott has said, "You will learn to dance with the limp."

Appreciate Your Transformation

The journey through grief is life-changing. When you leave the wilderness of your grief, you are simply not the same person you were when you entered it. You have been through so much. How could you be the same?

> "The only way to make sense out of change is to plunge into it, move with it, and join the dance."
>
> Alan Watts

Especially if you've made it through the early days and are a few months or more into your grief journey, I imagine you are discovering that you are being transformed by the experience. Transformation literally means "an entire change in form." Many mourners have said to me some variation on, "I have grown from this experience. I'm a different person." You are indeed different now. Your inner form is changing. You are likely growing in your wisdom, understanding, and compassion.

Don't get me wrong. Believe me, I understand that any growth you may be experiencing resulted from something you would have preferred to avoid. Though grief can indeed transform into growth, none of us would seek out the pain that comes with a suicide in an effort to experience this growth. While I have come to believe that our greatest gifts often do come from our wounds, these are not wounds we masochistically go looking for. I often call it "**enforced life learning.**"

When others offer untimely comments like, "You'll grow from this," your right to be hurt, angry, or deeply sad is taken away from you. It is as if these people are saying that you should be grateful for the death! Of course you're not grateful for the death. You would rather the person who died by suicide were still alive and well—and you would probably trade all the growth in the world for just five more minutes with them.

Of course, this isn't possible. You are grieving, and I sincerely hope you are authentically mourning. To understand how transformation in grief occurs, let's explore some aspects of growth in grief.

EXPRESS YOURSELF:
Go to *The Understanding Your Suicide Grief Journal* on p. 174.

Change is Growth

We as human beings are forever changed by the suicide death of someone in our lives.

You may discover that you are developing new attitudes. You may be becoming more patient or more sensitive to the feelings and circumstances of others, especially those suffering from loss. You may be becoming less patient with things that don't really matter. You may be developing new skills. You may be learning to fix your own technology problems or how to cook a nice meal. You may be arriving at new insights and decisions about how to live your new life.

You are new—different than you were prior to the death. To the extent that you are different, you can say you have grown. Yes, change is growth.

EXPRESS YOURSELF:
Go to *The Understanding Your Suicide Grief Journal* on p. 175.

Befriending Impermanence is Growth

Life is like a river. We are floating down a river that twists and turns. We can never see very far ahead. We can never go back. Sometimes the going is smooth; sometimes the rapids are rocky and dangerous. And sometimes a waterfall plunges us over the edge.

Life is constant change, which means the circumstances in which we love and are attached to things are also constantly changing. No matter how hard we try to manage risk and control our destinies, things inevitably happen that turn our lives upside-down.

Anytime we gain something new, we give something else up.

Sometimes we choose the things or people to give up. Other times they are torn away from us against our will. Either way, we're bound to suffer loss.

Love and attachment are indeed wonderful, but the circumstances of life are impermanent. The globe spins. The years pass. And things change. Then change again.

The journey through grief is in part a reckoning with the transitory nature of life. The more you come to reconcile yourself to the constancy of change, the more conscious you become. Yes, befriending impermanence is growth.

EXPRESS YOURSELF:
Go to *The Understanding Your Suicide Grief Journal* on p. 175.

Finding a New Normal is Growth

While your work of mourning will help you regain some sense of normalcy, it is a new normal. And as you work to figure out and accommodate the new normal, you are likely to try new things and stretch yourself in ways you didn't know you were capable of.

Suicide loss survivors sometimes remark to me that they never would have predicted their current life. As they set off to find a new normal, they got caught up in new interests and met new people.

But even for those grievers whose lives look more or less the same from the outside, there is a shift to a new normal inside. There is a new inner balance. Yes, finding a new normal is growth.

EXPRESS YOURSELF:
Go to *The Understanding Your Suicide Grief Journal* on p. 176.

Exploring Your Assumptions about Life is Growth

The death of someone to suicide invites you to look at your assumptions about life. Your loss experiences have a tendency to transform your values and priorities. What you may have thought of as being important—your home, your car—may not matter any longer. The job or sport or financial goal that used to drive you may now seem trivial.

You may ask yourself, "Why did I waste my time on these things?" You may go through a re-evaluation or a transformation of your previously held values. You may value material goods and status less. You may now more strongly value relationships.

As previously noted, when someone dies by suicide, you may also find yourself questioning your religious, spiritual, and philosophical values. You might ask questions like, "Why did God let this happen?" or "Why did this happen to our family?" or "Why should I get my feet out of bed?"

Exploring these questions is a long and arduous part of the grief journey. But ultimately, exploring your assumptions about life can make these assumptions richer and more life-affirming. Every loss in life calls out for a new search for meaning, including a natural struggle with spiritual concerns, often transforming your vision of your God and your faith life. Yes, exploring your assumptions about life is growth.

EXPRESS YOURSELF:
Go to *The Understanding Your Suicide Grief Journal* on p. 176.

Embracing Vulnerability is Growth

Grief makes us feel vulnerable, and we tend not to like feeling vulnerable. But it turns out there is great power in vulnerability. When we learn to embrace vulnerability in grief, we learn to be OK with expressing our deepest, truest feelings. We learn to openly share our souls with others. We learn to be genuine and authentic.

Stoic strength is actually weakness. Vulnerability is what's genuine, connecting, and life-affirming. In fact, one of the miracles of vulnerability is that it opens your life not only to healing but also to the potential of more joy.

To be vulnerable is to take risks to reach for what we want in life. There is no other way to get where we want to go. And even though we sometimes make mistakes and things don't always unfold as we wish they would, the rewards of embracing vulnerability are ultimately so much greater than the missed opportunities of staying closed-up and safe.

EXPRESS YOURSELF:
Go to *The Understanding Your Suicide Grief Journal* on p. 177.

Learning to Use Your Potential is Growth

The grief journey often challenges you to reconsider the importance of using your potential. In some ways, suicide loss naturally invites questions. Questions such as "Who am I? What am I meant to do with my life?" often naturally arise during grief. Answering them inspires a hunt. You may find yourself on a search for your very soul.

In part, seeking purpose means living inside the question, "Am I spending my time doing what I really want to do?" Beyond that, it means asking, "Does my life really matter?" Rather than dragging you down, your grief may ultimately lift you up. Then it becomes up to you to embrace and creatively express your newfound potential.

I believe that grief's call to use your potential is why many mourners go on to help others in grief. You don't have to discover a cure for cancer. You may volunteer to help out with a suicide grief support group. You may reach out to a neighbor who is struggling or devote more time to your children or grandchildren. Remember—we all have gifts, and part of our responsibility is to discover what those gifts are and put them to use. Yes, learning to use your potential is growth.

EXPRESS YOURSELF:
Go to *The Understanding Your Suicide Grief Journal* on pp. 177-178.

Your Responsibility to Live

Paradoxically, it is in opening your broken heart that you open yourself to fully living until you die. You are on this earth for just a short time. You move through new developmental and spiritual stages daily, weekly, yearly.

Sorrow is an inseparable dimension of our human experience. We suffer after a loss because we are human and we are privileged to give and receive love. And in our suffering, we are transformed. While it hurts to suffer the loss of people in our lives, the alternative is apathy. Apathy literally means the inability to suffer, and it results in a lifestyle that avoids human relationships to avoid suffering.

Perhaps you have noticed that some people die a long time before they stop breathing. They have no more promises to keep, no more people to love, no more places to go. It is as if the souls of these people have already departed. I encourage you to not let this happen to you.

Yes, you have to do your work of mourning and discover how you are changed. You have to live not only for yourself but also, I believe, for the precious person in your life who has died by suicide —to work on their unfinished work and to realize their unfinished dreams. I truly believe that those who die before us live on through us, in our actions and our deeds. When we honor their unfinished contributions to the living world, our dead live on. When we dedicate ourselves to helping others who come to know grief, they live on.

If, on the other hand, you have in any way set your intention to live in pessimism and chronic sorrow, you are not honoring your grief, you are dishonoring the life and death of the person who died. What if the person who died could see what you are doing with your life? Would they like how you have been transformed? Would they be proud of you?

What if they could see that you have mourned but also gone on to help others in grief and sorrow? What if they could see that they left their love forever in your heart? What if they could see that you live your life with passion in testimony to them?

No matter how deep your sorrow or how anguished your soul, grief does not free you from your responsibility to live until you die.

EXPRESS YOURSELF:
Go to *The Understanding Your Suicide Grief Journal* on pp. 178-180.

Nourishing Your Transformed Soul

Yes, your soul has been transformed by the suicide death of someone in your life. Your soul is not a physical entity; it is everything about you that is not physical—your values, your identity, your memories, even your sense of humor. Naturally, grief work impacts your soul! I often say that grief work is soul work.

In part, nourishing your grieving soul is a matter of surrendering to the mystery of grief. As I noted in the beginning of this book, real learning comes when we surrender: surrender our need to compare our grief (it's not a competition); surrender our self-critical judgments (we need to be self-compassionate); and surrender our need to completely understand (we never will). My hope is that the contents of this book have nourished your grieving soul.

There are, of course, many ways to nourish your grieving soul. Here are some that work for me. I nourish my soul...

- By attending to those things that give my life richness and purpose.
- By trying to fulfill my destiny, by developing my soul's potential.
- By striving to give back what others have given to me.
- By learning to listen to what is going on around and within me to help me decide which direction I need to go.
- By having gratitude for family and friends.

- By observing what is requesting my attention and giving attention to it.

- By finding passion in ministering to those in grief.

- By going out into nature and having gratitude for the beauty of the universe.

- By praying that I'm living on purpose and using my gifts, whether by writing a book, teaching a workshop, or caring for my grandchildren.

- By setting aside time to go into exile and be by myself in stillness.

- By earning my living doing something I love.

- By going through my own struggles and griefs and realizing that it is working through these wounds that helps unite me with others.

How do you nourish your transformed soul? What can you do today—and each and every day henceforth—to pay homage to your transformation? How do you most authentically live your transformed life? These are the questions of your present and future life. It is in honoring these questions that you appreciate your transformation and live the best life you can.

EXPRESS YOURSELF:
Go to *The Understanding Your Suicide Grief Journal* on p. 180.

Doing the Work—Today and Tomorrow

Depending on where you are in your grief journey, you may not be ready to fully engage with or feel inspired and encouraged by the contents of this touchstone. Yet even if this is the case for you, I believe it can help you hold onto hope for what can and will be if you continue to do the hard work of active, authentic mourning.

If you're beginning to experience and embrace glimmers of transformation, I encourage you to continue the intentional grief work you are doing.

Bearing witness to how suicide loss survivors have been transformed has been one of the greatest privileges of my life.

Either way, you are where you are today, and there is more work to be done tomorrow. The sun will rise again, and with the new day will come new opportunities.

Yes, out of the dark and into the light!

A Final Word

Thank you for stepping through this book with me. I hope it has been a helpful companion for you as you have worked to understand, embrace, and express your grief. Depending on where you are in your grief journey, I encourage you to reread it (or parts of it) from time to time. You will find that your insight changes and deepens over the course of months and years.

If you have also found journaling about your grief helpful, I urge you to keep going with that as well. If you feel like you are well on your way to reconciling your grief, you may want to move on to gratitude journaling instead.

When all is said and done, you love and you grieve. You grieve and you love.

I invite you to remember the power of "and" as you live your one precious life from here forward. It may help you choose to be present, to live with intention and action, to seek joy and transformation.

Whenever you feel stuck, whisper to yourself:

I am grieving AND I am present to all that is good in my life.

I feel lost AND I am finding my way.

I miss the person who died AND I choose joy.

I am bereft AND I am actively loving others in my life.

I grieve AND I love.

I love AND I mourn.

You have learned to watch for trail markers in your grief. Now learn to watch for trail markers in your continued living. Listen to the wisdom of your inner voice. Make choices that are congruent with what you have learned on your journey.

I hope we meet one day.

THE SUICIDE LOSS SURVIVOR'S BILL OF RIGHTS

Someone in your life has died by suicide. Your grief is unique and profound, and you have vital needs that must be tended to in the coming weeks, months, and years. Though you should reach out to others as you do the work of mourning, you should not feel obligated to accept the unhelpful responses you may receive from some people. You are the one who is grieving, and as such, you have certain "rights" no one should try to take away from you.

The following list is intended both to empower you to heal and to decide how others can and cannot help. This is not to discourage you from reaching out to others for help, but rather to assist you in distinguishing useful responses from hurtful ones.

1. **I have the right to experience my own unique grief.**
   No one else will grieve this death in exactly the same way I do. So, when I turn to others for help, I will not allow them to tell me what I should or should not be thinking, feeling, or doing.

2. **I have the right to talk about my grief.**
   Talking about my grief and the story of the death will help me heal. I will seek out others who will allow me to talk as much as I want, as often as I want, and who will listen without judging. If at times I don't feel like talking, I also have the right to be silent, although I understand that bottling everything up inside will prevent my healing.

3. **I have the right to feel a multitude of emotions.**
   Confusion, disorientation, fear, shame, anger, and guilt are just a few of the emotions I might feel as part of my grief journey. Others may try to tell me that what I do feel is wrong, but I know that my feelings aren't right or wrong, they just are.

4. **I have the right to work through any feelings of guilt and relinquish responsibility.**
   I may feel guilty about this death, even though it was in no way my fault. I must come to acknowledge that the only person truly responsible was the person who took his or her own life. Still, I must feel and explore any possible feelings of guilt I may have in order to move beyond them.

5. **I have the right to know what can be known about what happened.**

   I can cope with what I know or understand, but it is much harder to cope with the unknown. If I have questions about the death, I have the right to have those questions answered honestly and thoroughly by those who may have the information I seek.

6 **I have the right to embrace the mystery.**

   It is normal and natural for me to want to understand why the person I love died by suicide, but I also have the right to accept that I may never fully and truly understand. I will naturally search for meaning, but I will also "stand under" the unknowable mystery of life and death.

7. **I have the right to embrace my spirituality.**

   I will embrace and express my spirituality in ways that feel right to me. I will spend time in the company of people who understand and support my spiritual, religious, or philosophical beliefs. If I feel angry at God or find myself questioning my faith or beliefs, that's OK. I will find someone to talk with who won't be critical of my feelings of hurt and abandonment.

8. **I have the right to treasure my memories.**

   Memories are one of the best legacies that exist after the death of someone loved. I will always remember. If at first my memories are dominated by thoughts of the death itself, I will realize that this is a normal and necessary step on the path to healing. Over time, I know I will be able to remember the love and the good times.

9. **I have the right to hope.**

   Hope is an expectation of a good that is yet to be. I have the need and the right to have hope for my continued life. I can have hope and joy in my life and still miss and love the person who died.

10. **I have the right to move toward my grief and heal.**

   Reconciling my grief will not happen quickly. Grief is a process, not an event. I will be patient and tolerant with myself and avoid people who are impatient and intolerant with me. I must help those around me understand that the suicide death of someone loved has changed my life forever.

Helpful Resources

In addition to local resources in your community, these national organizations are good sources of information and support.

CONTACTS TO CREATE SUPPORT GROUPS AND ADDITIONAL RESOURCES
American Association of Suicidology (AAS)
1-888-977-3836
info@suicidology.org
suicidology.org

American Foundation for Suicide Prevention (AFSP)
1-888-333-2377
info@afsp.org
afsp.org

Alliance of Hope for Suicide Loss Survivors
1-847-868-3313
allianceofhope.org

Center for Loss & Life Transition
1-970-226-6050
centerforloss.com

RESOURCES FOR SPECIFIC GROUPS
Tragedy Assistance Program for Survivors (TAPS) - Military Families
1-800-959-8277
https://www.taps.org/suicide

The Trevor Project - LGBTQIA
1-212-695-8650
info@thetrevorproject.org
thetrevorproject.org

Suicide Prevention: Indian Health Services – American and Alaskan Natives
1-301-443-8028
ihs.gov/suicideprevention/about/

Boris Lawrence Henson Foundation - Mental Health for People of Color
1-213-222-6327
info@borislhensonfoundation.org
borislhensonfoundation.org

FOR IMMEDIATE HELP

988 Suicide Crisis and Lifeline
Call: 988
Text: 988
988lifeline.org

The Trevor Project – LGBTQIA Crisis Line
Call: 1-866-488-7386
Text: 679-678

Veterans Crisis Line – Department of Veterans Affairs
1-800-273-8255 ex 1
veteranscrisisline.net

INTERNATIONAL RESOURCES

Centre for Suicide Prevention - Canada
1-403-245-3900
suicideinfo.ca

Australian Institute for Suicide Research and Prevention (AISRAP)
+61-737-353-382
aisrap@griffith.edu.au
griffith.edu.au/griffith-health/australian-institute-suicide-research-prevention

Further Reading

Dr. Wolfelt has written many books to help grieving people. In addition to the one you're holding in your hands, you may be interested in reading others—especially those focused on your unique loss or experience.

NIGHTSTAND BOOKS
(to read for a few minutes in the morning or before sleep)

Grief One Day at a Time

First Aid for Broken Hearts

Stay for the Cup of Coffee

One Mindful Day at a Time

Healing Your Grieving Heart

The Journey through Grief

Loving from the Outside In, Mourning from the Inside Out

Eight Critical Questions for Mourners

The Paradoxes of Mourning

Healing a Child's Grieving Heart

Healing a Friend's Grieving Heart

Healing a Teen's Grieving Heart

The Mourner's Book of Courage

The Mourner's Book of Faith

The Mourner's Book of Hope

CIRCUMSTANCES SURROUNDING THE DEATH

Understanding Your **Suicide** Grief

The Understanding Your **Suicide** Grief Journal

Healing a **Parent's** Grieving Heart

Healing a **Spouse's** Grieving Heart

When Your **Soulmate** Dies

Healing the **Adult Child's** Grieving Heart

Healing the **Adult Sibling's** Grieving Heart

Healing a **Grandparent's** Grieving Heart

Grief After **Homicide**: Surviving, Mourning, Reconciling

Healing Your **Traumatized** Heart (sudden, violent deaths)

Healing Your Grieving Heart after **Miscarriage**

Healing Your Grieving Heart after **Stillbirth**

Healing Your Grieving Heart after a **Military Death**

Understanding Your Grief after a **Drug-Overdose Death**

Expected Loss: Coping with **Anticipatory Grief**

When Your **Pet** Dies

OTHER TOPICS RELATED TO LOSS

You're Not Crazy - You're Grieving

The **Depression** of Grief

The **Dementia** Care-Partner's Workbook (by Dr. Edward Shaw)

Grief Day by Day (**grief rituals and ceremonies**)

The Grief of **Infertility**

Healing after **Job Loss**

Healing Grief **at Work**

Healing Your **Chronic Illness** Grief

Healing Your Grief about **Aging**

Healing Your Grief When **Disaster** Strikes

Healing Your Grieving **Body**

Healing Your Grieving Heart after a **Cancer Diagnosis**

Healing Your Grieving Heart When Someone You Care About Has **Alzheimer's**

Healing the **Empty Nester's** Grieving Heart

Healing Your Grieving **Soul**

Healing Your **Holiday Grief**

If You're **Lonely**: Finding Your Way

Living in the Shadow of the Ghosts of Grief (**carried grief**)

Nature Heals: Reconciling Your Grief Through Engaging with the Natural World

The **PTSD** Solution

Too Much Loss: Coping with **Grief Overload**

Transcending **Divorce**

THE UNDERSTANDING YOUR GRIEF SERIES

Understanding Your Grief

The Understanding Your Grief Journal

365 Days of Understanding Your Grief

The Wilderness of Grief: Finding Your Way

The Wilderness of Grief Audiobook

The Understanding Your Grief Support Group Guide (for group leaders)

FOR CHILDREN AND TEENS

Healing Your Grieving Heart for Kids

How I Feel (coloring book)

I Have Diabetes (coloring book, by Jaimie A. Wolfelt)

My Pet Died (coloring book)

Healing Your Grieving Heart for Teens

The Healing Your Grieving Heart Journal for Teens

Living with Diabetes: A Journal for Teens (by Jaimie A. Wolfelt)

FOR BEREAVEMENT CAREGIVERS

Companioning the Bereaved

Companioning the Grieving Child

Companioning You!

Counseling Skills for Companioning the Mourner

The Handbook for Companioning the Mourner

When Grief is Complicated

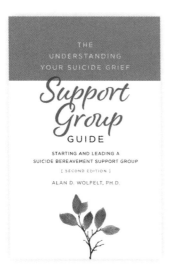

The Understanding Your Suicide Grief Support Group Guide

When we're grieving the death of someone to suicide, we need the support and compassion of our fellow human beings. Suicide grief support groups provide a wonderful opportunity for this very healing kind of support.

This book is for professional or lay caregivers who want to start and lead an effective suicide grief support group for adults. It explains how to get a group started and how to keep it running smoothly once it's underway. The group leader's roles and responsibilities are explored in detail, including communication skills, trust building, handling problems, and more.

This Guide also includes twelve meeting plans that interface with the second editions of *Understanding Your Suicide Grief* and *The Understanding Your Suicide Grief Journal*. Each week group members read a chapter in the main text, complete a chapter in the journal, and come to group ready for you to guide them through an exploration of the content. Meeting plans include suggestions for how to open each session as well as engaging exercises and activities.

ISBN: 978-1-61722-339-6 • 144 pages • softcover • $19.95

ALL DR. WOLFELT'S PUBLICATIONS CAN BE ORDERED BY MAIL FROM:
Companion Press | 3735 Broken Bow Road | Fort Collins, CO 80526
(970) 226-6050 | www.centerforloss.com